THE
ULTIMATE
DECEPTION

ALAN E WEST

Prime
"Your story is our priority"

LitPrime Solutions
21250 Hawthorne Blvd
Suite 500, Torrance, CA 90503
www.litprime.com
Phone: 1-800-981-9893

Published by LitPrime Solutions   08/10/2021

ISBN: 978-1-955944-04-5(sc)
ISBN: 978-1-955944-05-2(e)

Library of Congress Control Number: 2021917844

CONTENTS

CHAPTER 1

The Beginning

W here to start? To tell you the truth, I am so overwhelmed by the idea of telling this story! I don't know what to say first. I am greatly Impelled to do so in hopes that it may be of help to one in a productive way. I am hopeful to alert one not to be so naive as to induce drama and unhappiness into their lives by not listening to his or her gut feelings. One should seek help from the authorities for their loved who have mental or abusive issues rather than just hoping things will work themselves out. I am in hopes to help one to be more selective as to the company they may keep. Those whom you choose to surround yourself can either build you up or drag you down to ruin in a big way!

I myself have, unfortunately, been too naive, thus not listening to my inner self and common sense at times to my own demise. I had to learn the hard way not to trust the legal system. I made the mistake of marrying one woman with very bad morals and character. I also married another woman who had mental challenges as well as poor morals. She was very good at persuading the people who could make a difference to believe her stories over the truth.

I feel compelled to be forthright as to the factual events contrary to what others may have been told. These happenings that occurred were life changing and resulted in costs of tens of thousands of dollars and the devastation of the lives of those affected.

Despite the misgivings of my inner self, it is embarrassing, but it doesn't matter. I will rewind this story to the beginning which will explain why this author was turned against the abuse of alcohol and drugs and chose to never abuse alcohol or to even participate in the use of illegal drugs. The names have been changed to protect their identity .

In the spring, in a small hospital room in Liberal, Kansas, a small southwestern town with a population of 15,000 seventy five miles south of Dodge City, Kansas. Mrs. Wilson, whom we referred to as Ma, gave birth to her first son, Alan E West. That's me by the way. Four sisters preceded me. I never had the slightest clue of the immense trials and tribulations that were yet to come in my life.

Fast forward a few years, three years old. I was the youngest of five. Here is my first memory. We lived in Plains, Kansas, a smaller community, population of 1,500. It was twenty six miles from my birth home. My father, we all called Pa, was a sewing machine salesman and owned the local theater. He was a sure right fella to those who knew him. However, he did have a drinking problem.

For example, on one particular dark and eerie night, Pa came home after drinking. He had taken a motion to give my ma a beating. Ma picked me up and rushed me through the back door. She ran into the quonset shed to find a safe place to hide. We then stayed quiet for what felt like hours. After a while, after Pa fell asleep, Ma carried me into the house and tucked me into my bed. The nightmare was over, for a short time anyway.

Fast forward to four-years-old, everyone called me cottonhead due to my light blonde, nearly white hair. My Uncle Harvey, on my ma's side took a real keen liking to me.

One night, Uncle Harvey had taken me to a poker game at some drunk guy's house where there were several men in the kitchen. I'm not really certain whether Uncle Harvey was an honest man or not, but something had happened to make a guy mad because he was yelling at Uncle Harvey and went after his shotgun.

Uncle Harvey grabbed me up and ran us out the front door into the pitch dark night. I was really scared as I could hear a gunshot from behind, POW! Then another! We finally made it to the end of the block to his truck and away he sped in the opposite direction away from that crazy drunk!

Some time later, I remember riding in the back seat of our Ford station wagon, one with the wood grain paneling. It was dark outside, Ma was driving and Pa was drunk. We were just a few miles west of Meade, Kansas.

Pa started yelling and beating Ma on the head! I couldn't help but notice that there was a deep ravine right off the road. We inched towards that deep ditch with every blow to Ma's head! Then the car came to a halt thankfully! Pa didn't bother her much the rest of the way home as he passed out.

Right about the start of my fifth birthday, there were seven of us kids. My baby brother had just turned one when we moved from Plains, Kansas to Liberal, Kansas, seventy five miles southwest of Dodge City. My parents rented a house on main street there. I remember Ma telling me about the day she recalled inquiring about renting a two story house. The homeowner asked, "How many kids do you have mam?" Ma replied, "Seven." The owner came back with a reply, "THAT'S TOO DAMN MANY KIDS!" Ma then asked, "Which one of the seven do you want me to get rid of?" He rented the house to her after all.

Shortly after we moved in, Uncle Harvey stopped by to check the house out. My ma told him that I had been taking my wagon and tricycle all apart fixing things on them that were not broken. Uncle Harvey proceeded to take them to his farm to weld every part on them that would be removable. It seemed that I had a bad habit of taking them apart just to see what made them work.

The next day or two, he brought them back saying, " Alan won't be taking these apart any more. I welded everything that could come off of them." Boy was he mistaken! In no time at all, I would have them apart again.

My curiosity had gotten the best of me when a neighbor girl next door who I was in kindergarten with thought we would play doctor on the front porch at my house on main street. That didn't set well with her mom at all! She rushed over to my house and chased me with a long switch into the back yard where I ran under the back porch! I remember she was using some really bad language to me at the time! I sure wasn't about to come out from behind the laff boards I was hiding behind until she was gone! I was really scared!

After all the excitement and embarrassment that my ma had gone through because of me, my big sister Esther stuffed magazines in my pants in order to pad the switching on my rear I was about to endure. I learned my lesson really quick about that pants are no place for Better Homes and Gardens magazine! This really made Ma angrier than éver! She just pulled them from my pants one by one until she had gotten to the last one. Boy did I ever get a paddling!

That's about the end of what I remember in my kindergarten days, so I suppose we should move onto the second grade.

About the most memorable experience I had during the second grade was on one occasion, a sixth grade boy punched me in the eye right before lunch break at the school resulting in me getting a black eye.

When I had gotten home for lunch that day, my big sister, I will call Lorie, asked me, "WHO GAVE YOU THAT BLACK EYE?" I gave her the name of the boy who just happened to be in her sixth grade class. Upon her return to school that afternoon, she beat the living tar out of that big bully. I bet he didn't feel so tough after getting whooped by a girl!

CHAPTER 2

Fever

Soon after my eighth birthday, I remember it was around the fourth of July, my neighbor friend and I were doing what was considered cool for us boys back then. We were playing marbles in the dirt for keeps. Our favorite marbles were the cat eyes. We would make a circle in the dirt, put our marbles in the middle. We would then take turns hitting the marbles from the outside of the circle. The ones that we hit, we got to keep and take home with us. It was a lot of fun if you won the other guy's marbles.

After a while we thought we would mosey to the store and get a jawbreaker. On our way, we noticed a firecracker stand had burnt down. My friend commenced to shuffling stuff around finding a metal cash box. He picked it up and brought it with us. I didn't feel right about that at all because that would be stealing.

When we arrived at his house, he broke the box open with an axe. It was full of more loot than I had ever seen in my entire life! I told him I was going to call the police and give it to them. He reluctantly agreed so that's what we did. We weren't even offered a reward at the time nor were we even expecting one. It didn't even occur to us at the time.

Later that summer, I was diagnosed with a hernia due to a fall due to my standing on a barrel and slipped, thus racking myself. When I underwent surgery, I did not like the ether they gave me! I remember that horrible smell to this day, it smelled like brake fluid or something.

My brothers and I would always look forward for the church bus to pick us up for Sunday school on Sunday mornings and bible school in the summertime, I would share scriptures with the neighbor kids. I would read the bible to them telling them that I was wanting to be a preacher when I grew up. .

That same year, I was diagnosed with rheumatic fever, a terrible disease that came with excruciating pain in my joints and a nasty fever. I could smell that strong ether smell as I felt an electrical shock like in my boots. I also had pain like a heavy weight on my chest, and hallucinations that make Jack the Ripper seem sane. My ma was a maid at the Warren Hotel, and Pa was a milkman for the local Puritan Dairy. Both were at work the afternoon when a neighbor saw me in the front yard crying as I was thinking that there were snakes in my boots. She made the call to my ma and she rushed home from work and took me to the hospital. I was sick for two or three whole months!

I went to my Uncle Harvey's farm to stay with him and my aunt for a while. My other uncle, I will refer to as Ralph, lived across the road from them. My Uncle Ralph was an alcoholic also but he was a nice, funny drunk .

During my stay, he was so drunk that he accidentally placed a black cat firecracker from his messy dresser into his mouth thinking it was a cigarette. He didn't realize it until it went BOOM after he lit the thing! Boy, was he moaning from the pain! I'm sure it was painful but I sure thought it was funny!

I stayed on the farm for a month or so. I even got to drive the Ford tractor up and down the dirt road several times. One of the chores for me to do was to gather the eggs from the chickens every morning. I really felt sad when I saw my aunt chop a chicken's head off! It was running and squaking all over the place! It was good that I got to spend some time with my uncles although it would have been much better under different circumstances. I finally got to the point that I was feeling good enough for my uncle to bring me back home. I was really glad to see all my classmates again but I missed so much school that they made me repeat the second grade. I really did not like being held back at all.

My pa still had a drinking problem that turned him into a Mr Hyde. I not only was trying to keep him from harm or trouble most of his drinking days but was always having to protect my ma from him when he was on one of his drinking binges. I was pretty much used to it all as a daily routine.

One time Pa pushed her down the steep flight of stairs, I was so angry and really scared for Ma. I couldn't help but to punch him in the stomach as hard as I could! I felt bad that I hurt him. He used to get so drunk as to pass out outside where the mosquitoes were really bad! I stayed at his side through the night though. Many times I would be with him when he would pass out in the lobby of the hotel where we would sleep on the bench next to the elevator. He would always manage to go to work the next day though.

On one occasion while still living on the east side of town, the worst thing I did was to get caught smoking and playing poker with the older boys who lived across the street. They weren't exactly the straight up types to hang out with! That Saturday afternoon, Ma banged on the door. My brother and I knew that we were in Big Trouble! She whipped us with the belt and took our bikes for a week. I never smoked again, not even to this day. I really didn't enjoy that cigarette anyway because it made me dizzy. But I did miss my bicycle !

Once we had gotten our bikes back, I went over to Kim's house, this cute little blond from school, my first crush. I asked her if she would like to accompany me to the Saturday afternoon matinee, she said yes, I was bubbling with joy! So I told my brother Joe about my date. That rat ratted me out to Ma! She grounded me for another week. I really think she did so because my parents were having an overload of problems with a couple of my big sisters.

One of them, I will refer as Lorie, was fifteen or so, dating a thirty five year old married man with kids. He was always in trouble with the law for stealing radiators off of farmer's tractors. My parents were not too happy about my sisters lifestyle thus far, so it seemed.

One morning while I was with my pa, we arrived to the man's house that was dating Lorie. Pa confronted him about his relationship with my sister. The man wasn't home but his father was. I guess the guy's dad didn't like the way Pa talked to him about his son. He chased us off his property with a pitch fork! Boy, did we run to the car!

I was in the pervert's daughter's class in school . This girl was not very happy that Lorie was dating her mom's husband. The girl, in return, chose to take her frustration out on me! I was stabbed in my right arm while sitting at my desk by her. She had broken the lead pencil leaving the lead under my skin. She said, "That's for your sister dating my dad!" For myself, I decided to put love on the back burner for a spell.

Now other than having crushes on cute little girls, a little boy has got to have some hobbies. I'd grab me a length of rope and walk ten blocks down to the music store to look for piano boxes. If there happened to be any, I would tie my rope to it and onto my wagon and pull it all the way home. They were thin plywood boxes, pretty sturdy back then.

I would place one on the bottom open side up then I would lay the other one open side down forming an enclosed box. Then I would cut out a door and windows. Ma would come out into my clubhouse and sit at my desk I built helping me with my arithmetic. She was always helpful with my homework. I think that is the reason I excelled in math and English classes later in my life.

I was always the one fixing everything around the house. I remember one of my sisters would mess the screen up by crawling out the second story of our house to sneak on one of her late night dates. One guy she was dating was a guy that my dad didn't approve of. I saw him try to run my dad over in our front yard with his car. I think it was one of the guys that Lorie was dating,a preacher's son,that is. He was arrested for shooting out car windows around town. She never dated him again after that, thank God!

Another thing I really enjoyed doing was building a go kart out of grocery store produce crates. They would have a seat and a steering system I made with a rope. The only power was to have one of my brothers push me from behind. We did have a great time with them taking turns even though a wheel or two would fall off once in a while.

I was an entrepreneur, I would go door to door selling the Grit magazine which was a popular news magazine back then. I also sold The Daily Oklahoman Sunday edition door to door. They offered kids different incentives for more sales. Another product I sold was some kind of salve as well even though I was a shy kid, I was still motivated to earn money.

CHAPTER 3

Milk Route

Now, let's move forward a couple of years, I'm eleven. We had moved across town to the south side of town. My grandma who had been staying with us during her later years had passed away leaving my ma her farmhouse. They had it moved to Liberal, having it fully remodeled. Pa's still a milkman and I'm in the fifth grade. He ran the milk route sixty miles round, and much too often, he would employ my help, free of charge! At six in the morning, during the winter months, I had to get up to go with him. Sometimes it was so cold because the floors were all metal and the truck was poorly heated. It was so cold with the blowing snow helping him deliver his stops out of town. I remember my feet and hands would be frostbitten from such poor heat with the metal floors and the thin metal doors, I would cry sometimes.

I never asked for money nor did I get paid for my work, I was happy to get a bottle of chocolate milk or an ice cream bar or two for the day. I loved my dad and was glad to help him. All my hard work was for not, since I didn't learn much in school, although I did keep my grades up to average or above. I was a fast learner.and would usually power study the night before a test resulting in a pretty good grade.

Then, through the summer months, Pa would again employ me with no pay. I remember seeing the temperature as high as 116 degrees on the bank marquee. I might add also, there was no air conditioning in that truck!

Because we had no trees in our yard, when I wasn't helping my pa or was in school, I used to go across the street to the lake to dig up stray elm trees. I brought about thirty of them home to transplant. We didn't have a garden hose so I used a bucket to water the trees every evening. My ma and I would pull up the weeds and used butter knives to dig up dandelions quit a bit during those summer months. It was relaxing for both of us.

One thing I never stopped doing was building clubhouses. I would gather up used lumber and nails for the project by walking through different alleys. The nails were usually bent so I would lay them on a slab of concrete and straighten them out with a hammer. I built one with a hand dug basement and a loft upstairs. It was a great man's cave! I would sleep there many nights because my dad would get so drunk most nights sitting in the kitchen talking to himself all night until he would pass out.

Back to the milk route. I recall, one early Monday morning in Sublette, Kansas, Pa and I were on the truck. He had been drinking so much that he had passed out on the floor. I had taken the wheel to attempt finishing up the deliveries.

I continued to run the route as much as I could until I had gotten the hair brained idea to drive 15 miles to the west towards Moscow, Kansas where my big sister lived at the time. I will refer to her as Shelly, I had just gotten a couple of miles outside of Sublette when he had awakened and bashed me on the head with his fist multiple times saying, "You retarded nut! Where do you think you're going?" I flipped a u turn off of the highway going into the ditch as he was hitting me on the head with his fist! I managed to steer the truck back onto the road and headed back to Sublette. He Immediately took the wheel as we finished making the rest of the deliveries for the day.

Fast forward to seventh grade. At this time, Pa and I just concluded his milk route in Ulysses, Kansas. We were headed home, a 65 mile trip back to the dairy warehouse. Pa was driving the truck. All of a sudden he had stopped at the stop sign at the intersecting highway. Pa said, "Go ahead and drive," So what was I to do? He just laid on the floor going to sleep. What could I do? His company had gotten him a new milk truck, one that the gear shift was on the column next to the steering wheel, not at all like the old wagon. This one was one that you could drive standing up or sitting down. I had to drive standing on two feet, scared to death. It was in second gear all the way home while he slept! All this time I was hoping that we'd make it to the dairy safely without anyone from my school, which was on the way would see me as we would pass by. Fortunately, Pa had awakened before we had gotten close to the school and luckily, he had taken the wheel! Had any of my classmates saw me driving the milk truck, it would be known that I'd played hooky! I'd be in a whole world of hurt!

My brothers were pretty frustrated with me at times during the cold winter months. I was not a morning person at all. We had this wall heater that felt really good as I would lay in front of it every morning before school. It seemed that about every morning, I would almost make all of us late for school.

I always looked forward to gym class. One day, I was up glove to glove with our boxing champion in the ring. This guy was one lanky dude who had at least four inches reach on me and about six inches in height. Now when I looked up at this champion in the eye I thought, how am I gonna beat this Goliath? I had it figured out though, as soon as I heard the bell ring, I jumped straight up and delivered a jab right in his kisser! Boy did he bleed! Turns out that I knocked both his front teeth clean out of his head, fortunately they were just front partials. The coach stopped the fight at that point. That was that, there was a new boxing champion for this class.

Now, since I skipped so much school that year, the principal put me in advanced classes to challenge me. He told me that I was smart and by placing me in the accelerated classes, it would make it hard for me to miss so much school. However, it was to no avail. I still missed quite a bit but still made good grades because I would read up on the lessons the night and morning before the tests.

My pa was not able to make much money during this time due to the fact that he was too sympathetic to his customers on his routes. He carried eggs, bacon, milk, ice cream and cottage cheese. He would carry them letting them charge the goods. He was never able to collect for them at times because they would either skip town or not answer the door.

To help my folks, being I was the oldest of the remaining kids living at home, I would either go to businesses such as motels offering to shovel their drives in the winter months. In the summer, I would offer to sweep their driveways and sidewalks. I never spent the money on myself. I would give the money I made to my parents for groceries. They never asked for welfare at anytime or any handouts from anyone that I knew of.

I remember one thing about my ma though, she would always come up with a good meal even when we thought there was nothing in the house to eat. I don't know how she managed but she did. They were usually pretty tasty at that.

CHAPTER 4

Edsel

In the spring of my eighth grade English class, my teacher assigned our class a book report. She told us, "If you boys and girls don't get your book reports done, while all the other boys and girls are picking daisies, you will be in here writing your book report," I thought that was funny.

She did allow us to choose whatever book we wanted though. Now I really wanted to read a book and write that report but needless to say, I had no time for a lengthy read, let alone a detailed report on what I had read but I was smarter than your average bee. Wanna know what I did? I came up with the title, "The Day Daddy Came Home," I even made up the author's name who was a friend of my Pa's. My whole report was a sham and an abomination but my seed of deception had been sown in fertile soil. My sweet ole teacher liked my report so much that she gave me an A+ for an outstanding piece of work.

I was really too shy around girls for my own good. There was a cute blond haired girl who I had a crush on in the seventh grade. I would build up enough nerve to dial her number but when her mother answered the phone, I would ask to speak to the girl. Before she would get to the phone, I was so nervous that I chickened out. I would hang up the phone. I always felt like I should have talked to her but I was just too shy. I never did ever talk to her.

With my love life on standby yet again, I decided to get a job working for a man I will refer to John Gregory at his upholstery shop on Main Street. See, John was a lush just like Pa, the two of them were drinking buddies. He would take me to the bars telling them I was a professional wrestler from Amarillo,Texas! He would have the guys arm wrestle me. Of course, I knew no one believed that I was a professional wrestler but I never said anything one way or the other about it. I just smiled and was mostly embarrassed about it. I knew no one would believe the ridiculous story.

However, John actually taught me everything he knew about upholstery. I had gotten so good at the art that my upholstery class teacher would ask my advice about certain tips on some projects the class was working on at the time.

I was sixteen and walked everywhere I needed to go. One windy day, as I was walking home from school, I couldn't help but notice a large amount of greenbacks flying my way. A lot of people were running to catch this find. I, myself had no money of my own. I joined in gathering up the goodies and had gathered up a large wad.

I noticed a gas station attendant at a gas station had the misfortune of his wallet falling apart, I handed the man his money. I didn't know whether or not the other people returned the man his loote. He didn't even thank me. Nevertheless, I continued my walk the rest of the way home.

Later that month or so, a local radio station was having a contest. The requirement was that you either count or guess the number of call letters they had stamped all over the 1958 Edsel model car, The one that had gotten closest to the correct amount would win the car. Ma and I counted the letters up and made our entries. We entered many times because the rules allowed as many as you wanted.

When the day came when they'd announce the winner, I was walking by the car on my way home from school. I thought to myself, "I never win anything," thinking some rich kid would win it as I continued my walk home.

When I arrived home shortly after,there was a knock at the door, It was the radio station representative. I had in fact won that car! My very first car! Turns out the battery was dead and we needed jumper cables to start the darn thing. I was still just as happy as could be. The next day, the radio station interviewed me about the win. I was so nervous and did such a flub up in that sitting, the announcer told the audience that due to technical difficulties, the interview was not announced. Boy, was I relieved!

Now, my woodworking and upholstery teacher with his silly sarcastic laugh, would say, "Alan doesn't drive a car, he drives an Edsel, Ha,Ha,Ha." It always bothered me, but I just laughed right along with him anyways. I really liked that car.

CHAPTER 5

Rambler

One stormy night, Jim, chose me to drive him to the liquor store and back. I didn't really want to but less sane heads prevailed. Key in hand,we headed out the front door, and away we went to the liquor store.

Now, once John had gotten his bottle, we began the return journey. The rain was pouring down hard, I mean you couldn't see anything. I pulled out of the liquor store parking lot right in front of a white utility truck! The truck slammed into the broadside front quarter panel of ours, and totaled John's chevy truck!

The proper authorities were called and when they arrived, I was asked to produce my drivers license. The driver of the other truck was laying on the street as the ambulance arrived to take him to the hospital. I was placed under arrest, along with Jim and we were taken to jail. I was charged with failure to yield the right of way! I was booked and locked in the cell with Jim to spend the night. After a few hours, a superior officer had told them to release me as I was a sixteen year old minor.

It was embarrassing for me to see on the front page of the newspaper the next day! A picture of the other driver of the truck lying on the street in the rain. It really looked tragic!

My punishment was that every day for a month I was to clean the police department to pay fines and court costs. I was sure happy to have this ordeal over with at the end of the thirty day punishment!

Now I could get back to business with my school activities. See I'm a pacifist of sorts but don't take that to mean that I'm a wuss. I got a heart beating in my chest, and it's pumpin' hot blood. Anyone that comes at me swingin' later wished they hadn't. This particular day, in gym class, we were wrestling. There was this one kid in particular that sure had a mouth on him. Now I can't recall his name, but anyone you ask would be able to recall the look on his smug face that day when I lifted him high up over my head horizontally like he weighed nothing. There were shouts of, "No Alan, don't!" Echoing in my ears.

It was almost as if I couldn't even hear them until I heard the thud of him hitting the mat. Don't worry though, he wasn't hurt. We had really thick wrestling mats.

My brothers, I will refer to as Joe and Glen, would start about as much trouble as they could. Without fail, every single time that they would get into a fight they would tell the guy they were going to get me to come to their rescue. As soon as I showed up, there would be no more fighting. I would not even have to throw a punch. I'd stand eye to eye with a mean glare into their eyes. They would leave my brothers alone going their way home without incident.

During my teenage years, my brothers and I would drag main street until late into the night. Back then, that was the cool thing to do in Liberal. We'd bring our friends with us and just have a good time. Our friend who we called Bub would drive with Joe in the front passenger seat and me in the back seat with Glen.

Now there were these tough guys, you know the type with a really bad reputation. One night they pulled up beside us poking fun at my brother. It happened to be because Joe was drinking his soda pop from a straw. Joe was a golden glove boxer with all kinds of trophies. These guys wanted to meet us at the gas station on the south edge of town. The station was closed at that time of the night is why they picked that spot to duke it out.

They didn't waste any time going after it. Shortly after we had gotten there, one guy had put Joe in a headlock hitting his head and face with his fist. I was thinking this whole fight was stupid and had no meaning. I had to break this one up before the cops showed up!

I figured, being we were on main street of all places, I needed to put an end to this right then and there! I walked up to the guy who had Joe in a headlock and hitting his face. I delivered a judo chop right to the back of his neck. Everyone scattered. They swore that I had hit him with a lead pipe! What they didn't know was that I would break a lot of boards with that chop many times in woodworking class in school. I also ripped phone books apart to entertain my friends.

After this encounter, we continued dragging main. Later on into the night, some guys pulled up next to us on main street and asked if we wanted to go to a gang fight later. We replied, "No, we weren't into that." Now, little did we know that it was us that the guys we'd just whooped was wanting to get back at us for what I did to that guy!

Later, we were cruisin' down Walnut street on our way home for the night in my little Rambler. There were a whole lot of guys standing, blocking the street to prevent our passage surrounding my car, bringing it to almost a complete stop.

At this point, I wasn't going to take this crap, so I said, "Either they get outta the way or they are getting run over!" I shifted the gear into low and hit the gas. They scattered, jumping into their cars to follow us. I raced through the church parking lot right between the church and the house next to it faster than I ever thought my little Rambler could even go! We left them out of site!

Turns out that the guy I judo chopped swore up and down that I took a lead pipe and struck him with it. Later that year, his brother had told my brother, Joe that I had used a lead pipe on his brother. Contrary to what he thought, It was just my hand. I would not resort to such a thing.

My brothers, as much as I loved them could really be a pain in the butt at times. I would do anything for them and I know they would have done the same for me as well. Advancing forward into that winter, I was at home one Saturday night when the telephone rang. Ma answered it and called me to the phone.

Lo and behold! Who other than my brother Joe would it had been? It was Joe alright. He and Glen as well as their friend Nick had taken a notion to hop a freight train heading west to New Mexico to pay a visit to their aunt, I will refer to as Esther and uncle, I will refer as Lauren.

It was midnight and had been snowing all day long. The problem my brothers ran into was that they all three had jumped off the train eighty miles away in a small town in Texas! They thought they were in New Mexico. They had no one else they could think of to come after them other than me. I didn't like the idea of driving that far in the snow but I felt like that was the thing I had to do. I made the trip down there with no problems and they were sure happy to see me drive up.

They all jumped into my little Rambler and off we headed toward home to Liberal. I was careful not to drive too fast because of the snow. We were about fifteen miles up the road when all of the sudden I hit a patch of ice. The car went into a tailspin. We found ourselves traveling backwards looking at the front end of a semi truck which was coming right towards us. Luckily we ended up in between two fence posts and a parked car at a roadside park without hitting a thing. Boy, that was quite a thriller!

We were very thankful when we made the trip successfully back home. We were all very exhausted and went right to sleep.

As the winters in Kansas don't last too long, We always looked forward to the spring and summer months and we shall now advance onto the next summer of this story.

My job was a janitor at a local nursing home and that was how I was paying the bank note on my Rambler. I had gotten to the last loan payment this summer and was sure proud of that car. I had just washed it before I called it a night on that summer Saturday night.

I got up out of bed that Sunday morning and went out to my car to go to the store. As I sat down, I couldn't help but notice there were beer bottle caps strewn across the floorboard. Although I was not too happy about it, I placed the key in the ignition and gave it a turn. The motor sounded like a tractor and smelled like a freight train wIth pitch black smoke engulfing the car and the street! I was so frustrated that I went around to the back of the car and lifted the entire rear end of that rambler in the air. Ma later that day told me she saw the back wheels off the ground.

I proceeded to hide behind the house waiting for Joe to get home. As soon as he pulled up with his buddies, no sooner than he had gotten out of their car, I went running straight for him. I grabbed him and threw him up so high in the air that when he hit the ground he said he saw the shingles of the roof of the house! The quarrel made its way into the house as he ran inside and on into the bathroom, slamming the door behind him. I managed to force the door open making my way inside. He was ready for me, we wrestled to the floor next to the bathtub. He had a phillips head screwdriver in his hand and stabbed me in the left leg with it! "OUCH!" I yelled, "You ruined my new jeans!" as blood gushed from my leg. I was more concerned about my new tan denim jeans than the pain.

I chased him to the front door. My pa had taken a broom and swung it at Joe's head, missing him as Joe fortunatly ducked just in the nick of time! The broom had broken the screen door right off the hinges.

I grabbed ahold of Joe, threw him into the air, and before he hit the ground I gave him a judo chop to the back of his neck. I thought that I had killed him because it knocked him out. I was relieved that he turned out to be ok. I felt really bad that I hurt him so bad over a car! Even though he did me wrong, I loved my brother.

Turns out that Joe and his friends had gone to Guymon, Oklahoma, a town about 40 miles away to get them some beer. They seemed to have gotten lost booze cruisin' on the back roads on their way back to Liberal. The reason the engine blew up was because they didn't bother to check the oil before they left on their journey.

Joe promised to pay for another engine and a mechanic to install it. He bought me an engine for fifty dollars, but his shifty mechanic never showed. That fifty dollar engine just sat in the backyard until I had to have the car and unused engine hauled away. Because of my love of my brother, I just called it even and let bygones be bygones. That Rambler never ran again. I figured it shouldn't have been using that much oil in the first place.

CHAPTER 6

Twisted Affairs

I am still in high school, I started a new job as a maintenance man at a nursing home. My responsibilities were to keep the halls clean and do minor repairs and maintenance of the building. I also enjoyed visiting with most of the residents at the facility.

One particular resident, I will call Mrs.Jones, had a bad crush on me. She had dementia and a shaky stutter. She was a sweet little lady who stood about five foot one and probably weighed eighty five lbs. Mrs. Jones was thinking I was her long lost husband. While I would be running the floor buffer or mopping the hallway, she would grab ahold of me, trying to kiss me on the lips saying she loved me. I would quickly turn my head so she would get me on the cheek. The nurses all kept entertained as they observed the ordeals.

On one occasion, the administrator came to me saying that someone had been breaking in at night stealing large amounts of meat and canned foods. I rigged up an alarm system on the back gate to the kitchen to catch the culprit. The administrator and the other worker sat across the road in the field with their pistols as I was stationed on the roof of the facility with my pistol waiting for the thieves to show. They never did show up that night or the next. The boss finally told us that we would continue the episode another day.

It turned out that it was discovered that the nursing home food thieves were the

17

administrator and his wife absconding all the grub! Needless to say, they no longer were employed with the facility any longer!

As I mentioned earlier, I was pretty good with electronics, I had done some work for a television repairman who taught me some of his tricks of the trade.

I liked my job pretty well and enjoyed being around the old timers. There were a couple of nurses working there though that I wished I hadn't associated with. I was only seventeen and had never been to bed with a girl. A lot had to do with the fact that deep down, I was too shy and was reluctant to approach women who I would be attracted to.

One evening, they asked me if I would ride to Hugoton, Ks. with them on an errand in case they would have car trouble. I said "Sure, I'd be glad to." These ladies were in their mid twenties and a little wild. On the way back to Liberal, one of them kept sticking her wet finger in my ear. I said to her, "Stop it" she kept on anyway. It sure wasn't turning me on. For one thing, neither one was anything to look at as far as I was concerned.

As soon as we had gotten back to town, the one who kept putting her wet finger in my ear says, "Let's go by my house for a bit, I need to get something." The three of us went inside, she poured all of us a coke with whisky in it. It was pretty strong! Shortly after, the other lady had disappeared. She had left me there with the woman with the wet finger. It wasn't long when she tried to get me in the bedroom for my first time for sex! I was really happy when her friend returned to pick her up!

A few months later, one of the cnas, a cute little blond, I'll call Sally was a little aggressive towards me. Sally got wind from a lady who worked in the kitchen that I fixed her television so she asked me to come over to her little house to look at repairing hers. She explained to me that she and her husband were separated and didn't know anything about how to get it working. I was glad to come over to look at her tv for her.

I commenced to mosey over to her studio little house which was in an alley. No sooner than I knocked on the door, as she opened the door, she gave me a passionate kiss right on the kisser! To me, back then, I was a stupid kid thinking that her being separated was the same as being divorced . This is one time I should have run while I had the chance as you will discover later in this chapter.

As I was only seventeen years old, she was a few years my senior and I learned later, her husband was twenty eight years old and a tough looking dude who drove a mean, pink Thunderbird with loud pipes.

We continued seeing each other pretty frequently. She kept explaining how her husband was abusive to her and used drugs in order to get my sympathy. Of course it worked for a young guy that used his hormones to think with rather than his brain. That is what I was doing to say the least.

Her husband carried a pistol and he would show up in his pink T Bird roaring loud pipes as a warning to me that he was near. One day, he came knocking on my door at my parents house where I was living. He asked,"Did you take my gun from my car?" I replied "Yes I did." He then asked "what did you do with it?" I replied "I sold it." He then asked, "What did you do that for?" I replied, " I didn't want you to be shoot me with it!" He then turned around shaking his head in dismay as he walked away to his car, thus speeding away.

Sally and I continued the relationship for a while longer. I recall the last encounter I had with her husband was when I came over to her new apartment. I walked into the kitchen's back door, noticing him sitting on the couch in the front room.

He had just gotten back to town by hitchhiking for some reason from a town a hundred miles away. He was not living at this apartment or had he ever. He abruptly stood up saying. "I had enough of you!" and he started pacing towards me with his fists clenched as to throw a punch at me. I punched a hole through the wall with my fist from the kitchen into the living room along with a loud "GERRR." He ran out of the front room and I have never seen the site of him again.

I do not understand why I was so naive to continue that relationship! I was getting suspicious that she was carrying on a sexual relationship with my little brother Glen. She even asked me if she could show him her big boobs! I replied, " Hell no!" How naive I was to stay with such a slut!

One evening, I accused Sally of carrying on with Glen while she, my mother, Glen and I were sitting at the kitchen table. She stormed out the door of my mother's house mad as hell, taking off walking! My mother even was angry over the perverted suggestion that I would have accused Gien of such a thing. My brother denied it all together! They all made me feel that I was wrong, so I let it go for then.

Later on, in the following days, my brother, Joe had just gotten out of jail for stealing beer over in Oklahoma. He had been in jail for several days and I was even more suspicious that he too was messing around with Sally! By this time, I had had enough!

The next day or so, I bought her a ticket for her to go to Los Angeles, California. That night, I called my brother on the phone and asked Glen if he had been messing around with her, he said "Yes but so did Joe! We both have!" I asked, "Why didn't you guys tell me? I loved her." Glen replied, "We didn't want you whip our asses, that's why!" I replied, "You could have called me on the phone, I couldn"t do anything over the phone." That of course, thinking back is rather humorous.

A few days later, Sally called me from California saying that she wanted to return if I would buy her a trailer house. I told her, "You just stay where you are!" I immediately hung up the phone.

The last time I saw Salley was in an 'R Rated movie, 'The Student Nurses.' She only had a part as a waitress. I never have cared to see or hear from her again!

CHAPTER 7

Amarillo by 'Mourning'

One day, I received a letter from Uncle Sam stating that I was to report to the bus depot at 11:00 am on a particular day the following week to Amarillo, Texas Army Induction Center for I was selected for draft.

At the time, the Vietnam war had accelerated dramatically. A lot of my friends were on their way over seas for their service to their country.

We left Liberal at at 11:30 a.m. that morning. The bus made stops at different small towns rounding up draftees on the way to Amarillo. We arrived at Amarillo that evening and stayed in the Capitol hotel downtown Amarillo,Texas.

That very evening, five of us thought we'd go see a movie downtown at the theater. When we approached the theater we saw there was a John Wayne movie on the markee. To be honest, I thought I was going into the John Wayne movie. To my surprise, it was an x-rated movie. The beginning scene, was a salesman who went into a lady's home to sell her some product of sorts. The salesman tied the woman's hands to the bed posts and her feet to the posts at the foot of the bed and proceeded to dress himself in her panties,bra and ear rings. I figured that was all I needed to see at this point. I told the guys, "I've had all I can stand of this and it is an insult to my intelligence, I'm going back to the hotel."

As I was walking back to the hotel, I noticed there was a coffee shop on the left on the way. I always enjoyed a piece of pie or cinnamon roll and a cup of hot coffee anytime of the day.

I went into the little cafe and sat down at a booth. I was the only customer in the building. The waitress looked at me real funny and I couldn't help but notice her funny looking nose but I did notice the pretty blue eyes and some nice legs! She wasn't bad looking at all, I thought to myself. What really got to me was the cook, the older man, who turned out to be the owner and an attorney who was her dad. The two of her sisters and one boy, her brother, from the kitchen were peaking at me. I thought what the heck is going on here? Why are they looking at me like that? The waitress says, "Who are you and where are you from?" I thought that was strange. I told her from, Liberal Kansas. She says "No you're not, you are from California! Who are you?"

Boy this time, I really felt like I was really somebody! I don't know who I was supposed to be though! After that ordeal, I proceeded to go across the street to the Capitol hotel and get some rest.

The next morning I was sitting at the restaurant in the hotel eating my breakfast and that same waitress from across the street came in to get some change at the register. She spoke to me asking that I might stop by later to her cafe before boarding the bus. I explained to her that I was to go to the induction center and get a physical and testing and I could stop by later.

At the induction center, I proceeded to do all the tests and the physical. To my surprise, the doctor told me that because I had rheumatic fever and had a heart murmur from my earlier years and I didn't have to be concerned about going into the Army.

I was told to report back to the center for the bus departure to our homes at 3:30 p.m. It was noon when I left induction center heading on over to the little cafe to say goodbye to the little waitress and drink another cup of coffee .

Lo and behold! At 1:30 she says to me, "There goes your bus, it is leaving!" I replied "No, I'm going to the induction center at 3:30, so I need to be over there by 3:15. " She replied, "That is your bus leaving now!" Boy was I mistaken!"

To my surprise when I returned at 3:15 to the induction center, they informed me that my bus had left at 1:30! I must have had my wires crossed! What was I to do? I was stranded in Amarillo,Texas and nowhere to go, I knew not a sole there except the little waitress, Alas! It could have been worse. Fortunately I had just gotten paid for my work at the nursing home so I had cash with me. I then went back to the little cafe, told the waitress that she was right, the bus DID leave!

Rather than panic, I decided to make the best of the situation, so I asked her if she would want to go have a pizza later that evening and asked if there were any activities going on in Amarillo we could go for entertainment. She said, "Yes there's a James Brown concert tonight. I asked, "Who's James Brown?" She exclaimed, "You really don't know who James

Brown is?" Are you from outer space?" I replied, "No, I do not know who James Brown is." She says, "You have got to be kidding!" I exclaimed, "Well,we can go to the concert and I can find out who this man is."

At my own expense, I paid myself another night at the hotel. Later that evening, Kelly picked me up at the lobby of the hotel. She had this eight year old girl with her, named Karie. After the three of us enjoyed our pizza, we continued to the Civic Center to the concert. We all had a great time and I learned that I did know Mr Brown from his music after all!

We didn't pursue much else other than a lot of conversation and a few kisses. Kelly did tell me that the reason they all stared at me at the little cafe was that she and her family thought I was her long lost brother from California. She went on explaining to me that her grandfather was the president emeritus of one of the largest banks in Texas and how all of her relatives were multi millionaires. To me, this was pretty much a good resume for this eighteen year old boy!

I explained to her that I was getting a bus home for I had to get back to work. I thanked her for a really nice time and told her that it was a pleasure meeting her and her little sister Karie, I never intended to see the pair again at the time.

A couple of days or so after my return, I received a call from Kelly. She was crying, she said, "You need to come and get me and my sister!" I asked "Why?" She told me, " My dad is being possessive and not treating me right, he thinks that you are a hick from Kansas!" I want to move there with you." Like a dummy, I told her, "Sure, you and your sister just grab a bus and come on up! " Little did I know what a mess was brewing ahead!

When she got to my little upstairs apartment in Liberal, we had a talk, she was smoking a pack of cigarettes per day. I explained to her that I did not like girls who smoked and to me, it was a turn off. She replied, "Then I will quit completely, this is my last one!" " More power to you if you do," I replied. Sure enough, she never smoked another cigarette for years.

Kelly did fess up to the fact that she was twenty nine and that Karie was her daughter of four of her children. She told me that her ex husband was a major in the Army in Germany and he had mafia connections in south Texas and one was a crooked attorney who represented him. She said she grabbed Karie from school while she had the chance. This was the only reason she had legal custody of the girl, she explained.

CHAPTER 8

Marriage 1.01

just completed my junior year of school at the time I had met Kelly. She encouraged me to drop out of school and take a G.E.D. She told me that I was really smart and would pass it easily without studying.

I immediately set an appointment to take the test without studying. Because of the fact that English and math were my favorite subjects I did well. The testing lady told me that I made the highest score she had ever seen as long as she had worked there.

I quit my job at the nursing home and went to work at a local grocery store where I could make more money.

Because we were living together and doing well, Kelly thought it would be a good idea that we should elope being that her dad thought that I was a hick from Kansas and the fact that no one in my family was impressed with Kelly. I figured what the heck, might as well!

We didn't go far to elope. We went to the next county over to Sublette, Kansas about thirty miles from home. She told them that she was nineteen instead of twenty nine on the marriage license. I said that I was twenty one. Now isn't that CRAZY or WHAT??

We bought a fixer upper house on the east side of Liberal that needed a lot of work at a cheap price. I had always been pretty handy at fixing things so managed to get it to be a pretty comfortable little home for us three. Shortly after, Kelly became pregnant with our daughter,I will call Rachel, she was a sweet little baby girl weighing in at 10lbs.6oz.

Kelly was pushing me to be a salesman. My natural disposition in general was of a shy person. I applied for a job that came up selling life and accident insurance. I was hired and they sent me for training for my license for several days in Hutchinson, Ks. I passed the test and was issued my state license to do business for the company. I was doing pretty well with the sales but just a few months into my job, the company went bankrupt. That was the end of that!

Soon after, I applied for a job with an Insurance company out of Chicago. I was hired on the spot and was told that I would be going to Chicago for a two week training class. They booked me a flight the following week.

I was ready to board the plane when Kelly tells me to buy the most life insurance from the airport vending machine that I could. I did just that before boarding. I dont remember for sure how much I bought at the time.

I completed my two weeks training class in Chicago and was ready to get home to get to work. I called Kelly telling her I was headed to the O'Hare airport to fly home. The very first thing she told me was, "Richard, you be sure to buy all the life insurance you can at the airport before boarding." Again, I did just as I did before, buying the max and finished my journey home.

I had to do extensive traveling with this company putting a lot of miles on my Cadillac. The very worst part of the job was the fact that they didn't mail out paychecks, I had to drive two hundred miles to be paid in cash every Saturday. That was just too many unnecessary miles to get a paycheck. I had no choice but to pursue another career.

Kelly brought to my attention an ad in the classified in the newspaper to sell educational products with a promising career. It turned out to be door to door selling Encyclopedias.

The speel was, I would knock on a stranger's door. When they answered, I was to say, "Hello, I am Alan with [Such N Such] Educational Corporation visiting with parents of the neighborhood." I really had made many sales and was promoted to sales manager after a few months but tired of it after a while. I thought I would look into another field.

I was hired to call on businesses in the tristate area to contract for the company to compile a list of delinquent accounts. I would mail them to the company back east for them to collect. They would pay me an up front commission for each account .

As the years progressed, I sold various products which lead me into selling vacuum cleaners door to door.

We had purchased a coupon book which had a coupon for a free carpet shampoo. A man arrived at our house to shampoo our carpet. The shampoo service was free if we would agree to let him demonstrate the vacuum cleaner he was pedaling. He gave a pretty impressive demonstration.

I was really impressed with the product and how much commission could be made on just one sale. He did talk me into giving it a try even though, at first I didn't think a guy could make a living selling vacuum cleaners. However, the salesman made me very curious. I proceeded to go to the office to apply. The owner put me right to work the next morning.

I worked with my boss as he was training me to demo the product door to door. The guy was kind of strange to me. He would drive the countryside as he and I would demonstrate the product to farmers, this was fine until he would stop his car on a dirt road, opened the trunk, pull a rifle out and proceed to shoot birds off the telephone lines.

That was enough for me. I told him that I had enough training and wanted to work alone. I set my weekly goal at what the average salary was at the time. I started out hitting my weekly goal the first day of the week. I was selling vacuum cleaners since I got up until dark every day. I would sell two or three a day most days.

I had fun working with a particular older salesman I will call Ken. He liked to solicit farmer prospects to demonstrate the vacuum cleaner to. On one occasion, he was demonstrating to a farm housewife. I couldn't help but notice as I watched, that he had a long burger hanging from his nose. I really wanted to let him know but just didn't know how to do it tactfully. Because I didn't want to cause him to lose the sale by distraction, I remained just observant and said nothing.

He sold the vacuum fortunately. As we got into his car, I said, "Ken, I hate to tell you this but you have a burger hanging from your nose." He replied, " Why didn't you tell me??" I replied, "I didn't know how!" Ken said to me, "You could have cleared your throat and pointed to your nose!" I couldn't help but laugh about it all the way back to town.

I had gotten to be pretty successful at selling vacuums. I sold so many vacuums that my picture was hung in other stores as top man on the totem pole in sales for the region. My boss told me, "You never miss a sale, do you? If you do, you always go back and get the sale."

Without notice, my boss with the company was promoted and transferred to a far away area. I was disappointed that he made no indication that he was taking the promotion. I was more disappointed when he chose to appoint my biggest rival I worked with to take his place. The rival even went to my sister's house and tried to sell her a vacuum by telling her no matter the price I offered her, he would sell for less! The guy's wife told me once that he started out the door with a gun to come after me but she stopped him.

I asked my boss why he chose the co worker instead of choosing me. He replied,"You are the best salesman of all, you never miss a sale and if you do, you go back and retrieve it. That is why I chose you to transfer with me rather than him." He did all this without consulting me.

Shortly after, Kelly and I bought a house, a two story fixer upper in Pratt, Ks. We moved there because it was a nice town and Kelly was good friends with my big sister, Esther who was living there.

I went to work for a pest control company in Pratt. I wasn't too fond of crawling way back underneath houses though. Especially after crawling under this old house out in the country. The crawl space was really narrow. My flashlight kept going off, each time I would bang it on the dirt, it would come back on again. I crawled midway of the house, my flashlight went off again. I gave it a bang on the dirt, Low and behold! When it came on, I was looking at a dinosaur looking critter skeleton with long sharp teeth right in my face! I backed out from under that house in no time!

I went inside the home and explained to people what I had seen. The lady said, "Oh, that was our cat Charlie, He strangled himself trying to get through the floor so we stomped him the rest of the way." I thought, poor cat.

I really was getting very tired of my job crawling under dirty houses as time moved along. One day, I had an accident. The chemical hose had broken and sprayed the chemicals uncontrollably all over me! When I got home, I told Kelly about the ordeal. She immediately exclaimed, "Oh no! You have no life insurance!" I wasn't too fond of her response for sure! She was too materialistic to say the least.

I went on to work the following day as usual. I worked a pretty long hard day and was tired when I got home. As I drove into the driveway, I noticed a car there from another county. Kelly greeted me at the door and wanted me to talk to a salesman who was at the house. Wouldn't you know? It was a life insurance salesman that she had called to sell me life insurance!

Not long after living in Pratt, Kansas, I went to work back in Liberal for a uniform rental company. It was a regular job with pretty good pay.

After working with the company for a week or so, the boss informed me and a lady, who also was hired that we must go to a local doctor who gives physicals for the company. The doctor just happened to be a homosexual who I had gone to for a cold before. I didn't see any reason for him to have me pull my pants down. After I saw him for the cold as a teenager, he would try to pick me up while I was walking from time to time on the streets of Liberal.

To make a long story short, I informed my boss that I would rather go to a different doctor and I would pay for it out of my own pocket.

My boss told me that I would have to go to this particular company doctor. He had the female worker and I drive over to this doctor's practice. As she parked the truck, she asked me if I was going in with her to get our physical. I told her to go on in and I'd be in later. I lied! I never went in. When she got back into the truck, I told her I didn't go in.

When we arrived at the company office, I told my boss that I was not going to that doctor PERIOD! He set me an appointment with a doctor of my choice and the company paid for the physical after all. I did not stay with that job though. They added a stop onto my route that was a beef rendering plant. I could smell that bad smell coming from the building a mile down the road. I tried to hold my breath from the time I entered, gathered up the laundry, gave them the receipt then hurried out the door! That laundry stunk the cab of my van so bad, I wanted to throw it out the door for it had to stay with me for forty miles to the warehouse.

A couple of weeks later, my boss asked me if I had made this particular stop that week. I replied "No" He asked me if I had made it the week before. Again I told him no. He then told me that I had better get it this week or else. I replied to him that I would rather pay him the lousy fifteen dollars that that stop brought in than to service that stop. When it was all said and done, I quit the job. I went back to work in door to door sales.

Forwarding to a couple of months later, Kelly discovered that she was pregnant with another child. Kelly didn't really take good care of herself during this pregnancy. When we had gone to my sister's house at the lake, she hiked up and down the steep cliff outside of the lakeside home. The last time she pulled this stunt was very alarming for we thought she was going to have a misscarrage!

Along about springtime, Kelly was about seven and a half months into her pregnancy. She wanted for us to hop in our camper on a thousand mile trip to see her mother down in Corpus Christi, Texas. I told her that I thought it would be too hard on her being that far along. Ignorance prevailed again so thus we were off to the beach in South Texas.

She laid on the bed in the camper most of the way with no problems. After we arrived, her mom and dad took us to the different islands and beaches. Her dad, being the port director and designer there, showed us the various ports he helped to develop. After three days of fun, her mother thought that we should leave. The only problem was that she was having her friends over to play bridge and wanted us to leave at 6:00 that evening. It would be a twelve drive in the camper but we could pull over and sleep anytime we felt like it being we were in a camper.

So be it, we left Corpus Christi at 6:00 pm, spent the night in the hill country outside of San Antonio. The next morning headed on up to Childers, Texas where we spent the night in the hospital parking lot because Kelly was having contractions. Fortunately, it was false labor so we headed the rest of our journey home with no problems.

It wasn't long when the ninth month came around. Kelly had gone into labor late at night. She had called one of her friends from church to take her to the hospital which was in another town thirty five miles away. Her friend was an older lady who was driving really slow. It made me nervous to follow them moving so slow, as Kelly was having contractions .

We made it to the hospital, they rolled her immediately into the delivery room. I waited in the waiting room as her friend was in the delivery room with her. After a long wait, the Dr. came out with tears in his eyes. He told me that the baby was a healthy looking boy weighing in at 8 lbs 10 oz. He told me that the baby breathed in fluids that suffocated him to death in the birth canal. What a really sad day to hear of this news!

We both were depressed about the loss of the baby. I was wanting a boy but on that Friday the thirteenth day, we lost him. Although we were depressed about our loss, life had to move forward. We did the very best to move onward to get life back to as near normal as possible.

Kelly was good at pushing me into making more money but the worst cook you could find. She would brag saying, "One nice thing about it is, when we bring a covered dish to a get together, we get to bring the entire dish back home with us." To me, it was rather embarrassing!

When she would call Rachel and I to dinner, we would almost run and hide. Sometimes we would just look at our food and lose our appetites. Rachel and I would go off to Mcdonalds for a REAL treat!

One time, my sister, Esther asked Kelly why she had cans of cat food in the cabinet for we had no cats. Kelly replied to her that she would make tuna casserole. She told her that I never knew the difference.

When Rachel and I would be sitting at the dinner table, she would have for herself a pile of raw hamburger covered with worcestershire sauce. I explained to her that it would be like going into a pasture and taking a big bite out of a cow! There was a good reason for Rachel and I to be pretty skinny, I must say!

If anyone ever stayed for dinner, you could be assured it would be a quick way to get rid of them. Really, if anyone stayed for dinner, they never asked for seconds. She would put coffee grounds in chili even! The one sure weight loss diet that worked.

As the years went by, she kept her word as far as not to smoke cigarettes any longer. She started putting a plug of snuff tucked under her lip instead. What was worse, she would try to kiss me! That really grossed me out, to say the least.

She had gotten to the point that she would drink a twelve pack of beer every night, getting drunk and started smoking her cigarettes again. I had nothing against drinking, I just had my fill of drunks my entire life and wanted no part in it! She had gotten to the point that she was cheating on me with many men, it didn't matter if they were married and had kids!

I made a homemade lie detector that I learned from a science project. My homemade lie detector was telling me she was lying about a few things. To give her the benefit of doubt, I got her confession after I paid a professional detective firm to give her a lie detector test. The detective told me she was lying about everything.

The detective told me that on a flight to Corpus Christi, Texas to visit her mom, she had a couple of affairs with various men on her way at various airport bars. She admitted all this to me only after the lie detector testing proved that she was not telling the truth.

Because she knew a divorce was brewing, Kelly asked her mom if she would fly to Liberal from her home in Corpus Christi, Texas to go to the bank to finance a new house for her on the north side of Liberal and let her rent it from her. Kelly's mother did fly up the next week. She went to one of the banks and filled out the application. The banker asked her, "Why are you asking for a loan? "You are worth more than we are!" Her mom went ahead and wrote a check for the full amount of the cost of the house to the builder. Her mother was ok to rent the new house to Kelly as the tennant.

CHAPTER 9

Divorce 1.01

It came to the point that divorce was imminent! On one occasion, a couple of swingers were wanting her and I to come over to their house. I was never into this type of life. The lady's husband told me that his wife really had the hots for me and wanted us to spend the night. Kelly wanted me to jump to the occasion! I replied to her, " Hell No!" She and her boyfriend who was married and a father of two small children ended up going over to the pervert couple's house to spend the night! I couldn't take this type of marriage anymore! It was not like we were even married.She was really obnoxious!

Another man she was having an affair with while living in Liberal was the last straw for me! The night I knew of the affair with this man, I was upset because Rachel was with them and I said some pretty bad things to Kelly about him. For fear of the words I had spoken, he called the police on me. A police officer had stopped me and my nephew Walter later that night. The officer asked "Do you have a gun?" I replied, "Yes I do, it's right here, I bought it from one of your sergeants." The officer told me that the man had called and said I had made some threats toward him. I replied, "All I told my wife was that If he came up castrated, I didn't do it." The officer just smiled as he handed me my license back. We both departed our ways without incident.

I had made up my mind by this time that I definitely wasn't staying married to Kelly any longer. When I told her that I wanted a divorce, she told me that she still wanted me for intimate relations and that this other guy had had his testicles blown up in Viet Nam. She told me that she just wanted him as a companion. Kelly told me with all seriousness, "If you stay married to me, you know you will be a millionaire!" I replied, "I wouldn't stay with you for a billion dollars!" I then said goodbye to her as I proceeded out the front door.

The next week, Kelly's mother came to our home from Texas to have a talk with me. She told me that I should not get the divorce from Kelly and that Rachel needed to stay with Kelly. She told me that I should not try to take Rachel away from her mother. I replied to her that Kelly drinks too much and was cheating on me with the lowest life people she could find. I told her that I couldn't be married to a woman like that and therefore I was going to go through with the divorce.

We were granted an emergency ten day divorce. The attorney told the judge that the reason for the emergency was that we owned several properties in other towns as well as Liberal and other concerns. Our divorce was granted ten days after we filed. The day it was final, she called me at my office and told me, "Alan, you are a free man." I was so happy, I could hardly contain myself! At least she didn't clean me out financially, she was fair. I must give her credit for that!

Soon after, she and the supposingly neutered man had gotten married and a year later, gave birth to a baby boy. It must have been a miracle!

Poor Rachel! Every time I would pick her up for our visitations, she would come running to my van with a joyous smile and arms wide open! Our visitations were to be only two hours duration from seven pm until nine pm every Tuesday and Thursday. In addition, we had visitation every other weekend .

Every time I would return Rachel, she would refuse to exit my vehicle! She would cry and cry at the top of her lungs the closer we had gotten to her mom's house. She would grab hold of my leg, crying with her arms locked, refusing to let go.

Kelly would come outside onto the front porch hollering to me, "Alan, you know you are five minutes past your visitation! You know that this will count against you in court !" Then, she would rush over to the van, grab Rachel as she hysterically hung onto my leg crying and kicking. Her mother forced her out of my van and into the house. This happened every visitation!

Even though Kelly's mother bought her a new house, she and her new husband had gotten a divorce. Her and Rachel moved to Amarillo,Texas. Her mother sold the house in Liberal. She Purchased another house in Amarillo for them to live in.

Kelly was single again and on many occasions would leave Rachel at home with different men of whom she didn't even know while she went out drinking! That was quite dramatic for a ten year old girl!

Even though she had moved to Amarillo, which was a two and a half hour drive from

Liberal, my visitation was still the same two hours duration. I would drive to pick Rachel up, take her shopping or whatever and the same thing would occur! When I brought her home, she would cry and cry and hang onto me. Kelly would say the same thing, "Alan, you are ten minutes over time, you know it will count against you in court !" Then, she would drag Rachel into her house kicking and screaming. Boy that was tough to see her cry like that! Shortly after, Kelly met another man there in Amarillo and started on marriage number four. As you remember, I was husband number two.

There was a weekend when Rachel had her visitation with me in Liberal. At that time, upon a short notice, Rachel's mom and her new husband shows up at my door. They were both drunk, wanting to drive her back to Amarillo, a hundred sixty mile ride. I exclaimed, "You are not taking Rachel with you when you are drinking!" They proceeded to try to push their way into the house. I pushed them out before they could get in, sending them on their way back home without Rachel. They were none too happy as they stormed over to their car and sped away!

Weeks later, one mid afternoon while I was in Amarillo. I was talking on a pay phone to my secretary about business. Kelly and her husband who had been drinking drove up next to me. I walked the few steps over to their Cadillac's passenger side window as I noticed that her husband had a 44 revolver sitting on his lap. Kelly had a beer in her hand.

He asked me, "Why did you push my bitch against the wall?" I was trying not to laugh as I replied, "I didn't push your bitch against the wall!" I was backing away from the pay phone to escape into my van as he had gotten out of the Cadillac he was driving. He headed towards me with the gun drawn. I immediately jumped into my van.

Keep in mind, this was on a busy street in front of a very large cafeteria! This guy was carrying a big hand gun heading behind the rear of my van! I couldn't help but notice a male customer leaving the cafeteria witnessing the whole ordeal. The patron ran as scared as hell the other direction away from the encounter.

The distraction gave me a chance to get into the driver's seat from the back of my van. I immediately jumped into the driver's seat, slipped the van into gear rushing over the median. I sped to the police station to report the incident! I never did, however, follow up on charges about this occurrence.

Because of the lack of care along with the neglect Rachel was receiving, I had contacted the Texas Children's Protection Services reporting concerns of my daughter's safety on numerous occasions. They told me that I should file for change of custodial custody for her own safety. I saw no other remedy other than to pursue making that change in the near future. I did have Kelly's sister who lived in Amarillo to keep an eye on things as well as The Department Children's Protective Services were aware as well.

CHAPTER 10

Naive Seduction

I was at the point in my life although I was deeply concerned for Rachel''s well being, I was mostly trying to get my life back to normal.

I was bringing in good income from my business downtown. I had an office employee who helped with the customers during the times I would be in surrounding communities going door to door making sales with my vacuum cleaners. When I returned at the end of the day, I would do the repairs that came in along with the book work.

I was making good money. I had my own house I was buying. I drove a Corvette, a two door Cadillac, and a customized van. I had plenty of money in the bank. All the conveniences I needed at the time.

I was dating various women but more or less not on a steady basis. I was very content at this time in my life, although I was not content with Rachel's situation in Amarillo at all. It left me with little rest when I would think about her circumstances.

In the fall, a year or so after I divorced Kelly. The regional vacuum cleaner office was having a sales meeting and a party in Dodge City, Kansas. The party was being held at a social club with a live band and all the alcohol you could drink.

I was still enjoying my single life and was in no relationship with any woman whatsoever at this time. Little did I know that the very worst castrathy was about to befall on my life. Just sitting at a table away from where I was sitting was a disaster waiting to happen.

She was the most beautiful woman in the building. I couldn't help but notice her pretty blond hair and her sparkling blue eyes. I have always been more attracted to blond haired women with blue eyes anyway. I reluctantly walked over to her table. I then noticed that she had a diamond ring on her left hand which made me think she was taken at the time.

As I sat down in the chair beside her at her table, I introduced myself and asked what her name was. I will refer her as Pam. I then asked, "What's with the rock?" as I pointed to her diamond ring. She replied, "It is to keep the wolves away." I replied, "I am not a wolf, what did you say your name was?" She again told me her name and said she was from a little town north of Russell, Kansas, about 300 miles from where I was living.

We visited for a while, she had several mixed drinks I noticed. We danced a few slow dances through the evening until I asked her, "Would like to go for a ride in my Corvette?" "Yes" she replied. We immediately left the company party.

When we had gotten to the parking lot, I had to admit to her that I didn't have my Corvette with me, it was at my house in Liberal. "That's ok," she replied. We went riding around in my customised van just the same. We were gone for an hour or so before I dropped her off to her vehicle at the club parking lot.

Before she exited my van, after exchanging a few kisses. I mentioned to her that maybe we should meet up sometime the following week about half way in some town between her home and mine. I told her, "We could knock doors together and sell some vacuums." Pam replied, "Sounds like a good plan!" I will give you a call!" We then went our separate ways home.

The Monday after, Pam gave me the call. She agreed that we would meet up in Scott City, Kansas where we could get a motel and could go door to door giving demonstrations of the vacuum.

The next morning, I packed my things ready to have a great time working with a pretty woman and making a lot of sales! I loaded my van with all the essentials and headed north. The drive for the both of us was about a two hour drive.

We both arrived at the motel late that afternoon about the same time. We unpacked our bags, visited for a bit, then we went to a little cafe to get some dinner. We drove around town a little, checking it out, Then headed back to the motel.

Pam explained to me that she had been attending college and telling prospective customers at the door that she was working her way through college by being paid for demonstrating the vacuums.

Later through the evening, she rolled up a joint. I explained to her that I wasn't into smoking weed but each to their own. She slipped into the restroom to do her thing with her weed. She came out from the restroom smiling and in a good mood.

As I say, she was in a pretty good mood, I'd say! When she came out, she sat by me on the bed, explaining to me that her family physician advised her that she wasn't able to get pregnant because she had too much scarring in her uterus. Naive me! A guy will believe anything a pretty girl says when he is thinking with his hormones!

The next morning, after breakfast we jumped in my van and headed out to the country to knock on some farmer's doors. It was pretty much a hot, muggy day, I must say. The two of us had knocked a total of five or six farmer's doors when alas! Pam knocked on one of a farmer's door whose wife happened to be home at the time.

Pam explained to the nice lady that she was demonstrating vacuum cleaners and vacuum her carpet for her. The lady replied, "Yes! Come right in My carpet sure needs vacuumed."

Pam rushed over to the van to get the vacuum and demo kit for this venture. I followed her on into the lady's house and sit on the couch to observe the demonstration. The housewife was sitting in her recliner to observe also.

Pam proceeded to take the vacuum cleaner from the box and assemble it for the show. She told the lady who was using the same brand of vacuum we were selling, "Let me see your vacuum that you have been using for a minute." The lady dragged her vacuum from the closet to Pam to look over, then told her, "I am going to check it over and let you vacuum this area of your carpet." I could not hardly contain myself from being upset for what I had just witnessed, She had disengaged the belt on that vacuum knowing that it would hardly pick anything up at this point. She handed the lady's vacuum to her and says, "Now, you vacuum this area until you think you have it clean." The sweet lady went over that area twenty five times. Pam then exclaimed, "Now, let me put my clean demo cloth on my vacuum and I'll clean the same spot! OH! Look at all the dirt yours left behind!" I was disgusted about the way she had gotten the lady to write her a check for the new vacuum cleaner after trading her other one in!

When we got into my van, Pam was so proud of herself that she had made the sale. I admonished her, saying angrily "What the hell did you take the belt loose off her vacuum cleaner for?" "If you have a good product, you don't have to cheat!" "Who the Hell taught you to do that any damn way!" She told me that her trainer from the company told her to do such a thing. I told her to never, ever let me see that happen again while she is with me!

I should have been smart enough to take the clue to not have anything more to do with this woman. First, she smoked pot, second, she was a chain smoker, third, she was a crook!

We knocked a few more doors out in the country where I had given a demo and sold a vacuum. We then went into town where I sold another. We then pulled up to a hamburger joint that also served root beer in a frozen mug. We placed our order for a sandwich and a rootbeer. After we were done eating, we had not gotten very far down the road as I noticed she had a root beer mug in her lap! Not only that, she ran off with the tray also! I immediately flipped a u and went back to the restaurant to return the items! Damn! I told her, "Never,

ever do anything like that around me again!" What a fool I was for even associating with this Chick! Believe Me! It gets worse! More than one could ever imagine!

After Pam and I figured we had a pretty successful day, we went back to the motel calling it a day around dusk. We were both pretty tired for it had been pretty hot that day in the Kansas Western skies.

When we arrived to our room, I would turn the television on to watch the evening news. Pam immediately reached for the phone, calling all kinds of people trying to locate some pot even though I had told her that I was not comfortable being around any illegal drugs. I had assumed that she smoked all that she had brought with her on this trip.

She was acting crazy, crying and acting all anxious! This went on for what seemed like hours. All of the sudden, after making contact with one of her friends on the phone, she jumped out of her bed and rushed out of the door, she told me on her way out that she would return shortly. She was gone for an hour or so, returning in a lot calmer mood.

I was thinking, what have I gotten myself into! I had about enough of this chick! The problem was for me was that she was too hot of a looking woman! Man! What an idiot I was not to run away the other direction!

The next morning, we made another sale and one in the afternoon. I must say that she didn't pull any of her shady tricks that day in her demos, thank God!

Early that afternoon we both headed back to our homes. I really was not wanting to have much more to do with this woman after this venture was over. So I thought!

CHAPTER 11

Choppy Waters

A week or two went by without incident. I was just living a normal life. I would work from the time I had gotten up until it was time to go to bed.

Wouldn't you know? One evening, while I was sitting at my office, it was about ten p. m. as a matter of fact. I received a call from Pam, she was crying! She was calling me from a motel room in her hometown about three hundred miles from my place.

Pam said to me anxiously, "My friends and I were here at the motel, the police came and there was pot here, they took them to jail! Could you please meet me halfway and let me follow you back to Liberal to stay with you at your house?"

What a naive, brainless person I had become! Thinking with my male hormones again! I replied, "Sure, when are you leaving?" She replied, "In fifteen minutes!" I said, like a fool, "I'm on my way!"

I reached the halfway point in the little town after midnight, and turned into the roadside park just on the edge of town. Shortly after, Pam pulls up,parking her car behind my van. She was pretty upset about the drama that had taken place that day but seemed really happy to see me again.

The two of us slept on the bed in my van for the rest of the night. At the crack of dawn, she got into her car and followed me to Liberal to my house.

It was obvious that she was an anxious woman. It really annoyed me how she would always seek out her favorite drug from different folks such as my renters who were potheads as she had discovered.

I was also annoyed that she would go into the bedroom, close the door and cry at the top of her lungs, saying, "Why me? Why me? I want my ma ma" whaaaa, waaaaaa!" This would go on for thirty minutes to an hour sometimes longer. What idiot besides a guy like me would put up with this crap?

Regretfully, after a couple of weeks of being together, we decided that she would stay in Liberal with me. I had my reservations of this happening anytime soon to say the least!

Because of her plans, she had me drive her to her mother's house where she had been living since leaving college. Pam wanted to gather some of her belongings thinking that it would be nice for her mom and I to meet while we were there. The drive was about four hours from Liberal.

It was a hot summer afternoon that day! As we drove up her mother's long driveway to their rather large country home, I could see her mom working in her large garden.

As we parked, I noticed her mom stooped in the garden. She quickly arose to turn to us as we parked. Her mom was a big boned type lady. I stayed put in the van as Pam stepped out hollering over to her mom saying, "Mom, I would like for you to meet Richard, he is one of my work associates."

I could tell that her mom didn't take a liken to me for she had a stern, mean look on her face. Her fists were clenched on each of her hips and her legs were spread apart as if she was in a wrestling ring!

I did not feel comfortable at all with that lady! Pam quickly gathered her belongings, told her mom that she would call her the next day. She told her mom, as she darted into my van that she was going to Liberal to work for me as my secretary .

I gave the ignition key a turn, backed out of the drive and raced on down the roadway to make my get away from that mad mama! Three hours later, we were back on my home turf for an adventure brewing that I would not dare for my worst enemy to experience!

CHAPTER 12

Psycho Mania

Liberal, Kansas, the land of ahs, Wizard of OZ, that is! Boy! Was I in for one hell of a ride on this journey as you will see in the next few chapters.

Pam and I had made my bachler house into a home that was pretty comfortable. She was a neat house keeper and a great cook. For me, as you were informed in previous chapters, Kelly couldn't boil water without burning it. We both worked at my shop downtown. She would wait on the customers who came into the store and I most generally loaded up my van with merchandise, drumming up some business.

I was making pretty good money and paid Pam enough to make her car payments and anything she needed. We got along fairly well as the days and weeks went by.

Then came a great obstacle in our lives! Although she had told me that she would not be able to get pregnant, WALA! Guess What? She thought she was pregnant! All hell broke loose from this day forward! I never, ever thought such a thing as this could ever bring so much chaos into one's life! Hang on to your seat for a crazy journey through this dramatic venture!

Pam was twenty one years of age at the time but was pretty much bonded to her mother. Pam had mentioned to me that her mom had put her in a cage while she would hang clothes and things such as that.

When she learned she was pregnant, she would go into the bedroom crying, saying, "Why me? Why me? What am I going to tell my mama? Why me? I want my mama! Whaaaaaaah,whaaaaaah!" She would go on and on and on, crying and repeating the cries for her mother.

Pam continued smoking pot, of course she was sneaking around to do so. She also continued smoking and drinking excessively. For a woman who was pregnant, I was not very happy about the way she was conducting herself.

As the months progressed, she still did not want the baby. She would go into the bedroom, crying for her mommy and saying, "I hate this baby!" Why me? Why me?" I want my mama!"

It had gotten so bad! One Friday night, about three am. We both were in bed for the night. I needed my sleep for I was to open my store at nine a.m. Pam called my sister in law, Amber . She just talked and talked as I was trying to go to sleep.

I told her that it was three o'clock in the morning and if she didn't hang up the phone or go to the other room, I would unplug the wall phone. She told my sister in law, "Alan says if I don't hang up, he will disconnect us! I don't listen to him anyway!"

That was the last straw! I unplugged the heavy wall phone. BAM! The next thing I saw were stars! She had broken the phone almost in two on my forehead. Blood was gushing from my forehead and my eye was swollen

Pam then jumped out of bed, ran into the kitchen. She pulled out the biggest butcher knife she could grab out of the drawer. She proceeded to latch onto the knife with all her strength, saying, "I hate this baby, I hate this baby!" She was trying to stab herself into the stomach as she was saying such awful things. I proceeded to try to get the knife from her. My daughter, Rachel,who was visiting was awakened from all the drama, she jumped out of her bed rushing to help me retrieve the knife from making contact with Pam's belly. Finally Pam lost her grip and in so doing, my elbow hit her in the nose, my hand had so much force as I succeeded to retrieve the weapon that she was using on herself and the baby away from her.

Pam ran out the door, jumped into the car, rushed over to the sister in law's house of whom she was talking. When she arrived, she rushed out of the car to tell Amber what I had done to her. She told her, crying as she spoke "Look what Alan did to my nose!" Amber said, "My God! What did you do to Alan?" I had my shirt ripped, blood was flowing from my forehead and my eye was swollen. Pam didn't have much to say after that.

I returned to my car that late night very tired, I then made my way back home to get some sleep . It would be hard for me to be able to open my shop at nine am that morning. Pam came home all settled down a little later that night without incident. I did manage to be able to open up the shop on time, fortunately.

As days and weeks turned into months, Pam still was very angry about being pregnant with my child! She would continue to smoke cigarettes, drink beer and sneak around smoking a joint when I wasn't around. She continually would gp into the bedroom and close the door. I would stand outside the door hearing her constantly say, " Why me? Why me? Waaaaa, waaaaa, I want my Mama!"

For example, one evening, as I walked into our house after work, Pam was crying and screaming, saying, "Why me? Why Me? I Hate this baby, I want my mama!" She had emptied all the drawers of our unborn baby's clothes, throwing them all about. She then ran, crying as she ran to one wall, banging her head against it. She then turned the other direction running to the wall banging her head against it. She continued this temper tantrum for at least fifteen minutes, screaming and crying that she hated the baby and wanted her mama!

Somewhere along the second trimester of the pregnancy, she was telling her good friend that she wanted to have an abortion because she was scared to inform her mother of the pregnancy. She would cry, throwing the same ole fits! why me? and I want my ma ma fits!

Pam informed me, one day that she and her friend had gotten her an appointment for an abortion in Hutchinson, Kansas and the friend would be driving her there for the abortion.

I did not go along with aborting the baby idea at all! I pleaded with her not to go through with the procedure! It was to no avail that my plea be honored.

I, after hours of pleading with her, convinced her to let me drive her to the abortion clinic in Hutchinson instead of her friend, thinking that I could pursude her to change her attitude.

The following Monday, she and I headed on the two and a half hour trip to the clinic. The entire time, I would say to her over and over, "Pam, please don't kill our baby, the baby is mine too! Don't do it!"

We reached our destination at the clinic. Pam went into the examination room with the Dr as I sit in the waiting room praying that she wouldn't go through with it. Thirty minutes later, she walked over to me saying in a tearful voice and cried, saying, "They won't do it!" They say I am too far along, we need to go to Wichita to have it done. They set the appointment for today." My joy quickly turned to sadness as we headed to the car for another miserable trip to another abortion clinic! For the entire sixty miles, I was trying to persuade her not to go through with the abortion!

As we turned into the clinic parking lot, I had a queasy feeling in my gut. Pam was very anxious and nervous about it as I was still trying to talk her out of her decision as we walked all the way to the receptionist window.

We both sat in the waiting room in anticipation of what would happen. About ten minutes later, her name was called to go into the examination room. My heart seemed to be skipping a beat from this sad happening. Judy got up out of her chair and followed the nurse into the room. I waited with great anxiety. Fifteen minutes later, she came walking out towards me as she was crying, saying, "I just couldn't go through with it!" I was happy with the news. I took her by the hand and on we went on our two hundred thirty mile trip home!

Not every day was drama however. Pam and I would go to friends and relative's homes in the evenings. We would play a few hands of poker or different board games. We both enjoyed these activities as well as a round or two of crochet.

Along about Pam's trimester of her pregnancy, we were over at my brother Joe and his wife's house, just visiting. Everyone was drinking beer and I was drinking my coffee. My brother in law, Lauren, whom I always respected and looked up to, said to me privately, "Alan, let's go for a ride, I want to talk with you. " I replied, " Sure, let's go."

The two of us got into my corvette. Soon after we left my brother's house, he says to me, " Alan, Pam is really getting close to nine months in her pregnancy. You don't want to be a jerk and have a bastard baby do you?" I replied, "Well… ., not really, but she is crazy and she is really wild and not a ready the settle down type of woman, I want to do the right thing though." I told him I would have to think about it. We then returned to my brother's house to resume the association for that evening. Shortly after, we all went our separate ways for the night.

CHAPTER 13

911 Elope

The following week or so, I did a little thinking about what my brother-in-law had talked to me about concerning having a bastard child. This haunted me and my conscience. I did not want to be a jerk and I wanted to do the right thing. In order to do this right thing, I began initiating a plan to marry Pam. She was in the seventh month of pregnancy, so I had to do something fast!

The next few days Pam and I decided that we would go to Clayton, New Mexico where we could be married, getting the blood test all in one day.

We left the next morning for the hundred fifty mile journey. When we arrived at the Justice of the Peace's office at the little courthouse, the worker there had gotten pretty excited when she saw Pam. The lady told us that we would need to go across the street to get a blood test. This we did right away.

Pam and I rushed back over to the Justice of the Peace's office and told the lady that we wanted to get a marriage license for we needed to get married that very day! She Immediately grabbed the phone to call the judge who just happen to be out walking his dog. She told him, "Your honor, we have an emergency! We have a couple here who want to get married right away! She's about to have a baby any minute, could you hurry over here and marry them please?"

We had already had a blood test done and the license, so that is all we were waiting for. It was ten minutes after the call, in pops the judge with his little dog on a leash.

The judge abruptly, jokingly, says, "This IS an emergency! Let's get you two hitched up right away before she goes to the delivery room!"

The judge had gotten us hitched up in no time at all. He then continued his walk with his little dog. For Pam and I, we slipped into my Corvette and headed east to the lake at Dalhart,Texas to meet up with my big sister and her husband, Lauren. He was the one who convinced me to marry Pam in the first place.

This was as much of a honeymoon we could do being that Pam was so far along in her pregnancy.

The day soon turned into night, it had been a long, tiring day. Pam and I called it a day, thus checked into a motel in Dalhart.

We no sooner cuddled up in our bed when we heard a knock at the door. Tap! Tap! Tap! Wondering who would be knocking at such a late hour of the night, I eased myself out of bed, wrapping myself with the blanket . I gently opened the door part way to take a peek. It was none other than Esther"s teenage son, Wilbur! He asked, as I slowly open the door, " Hey Uncle Alan, I hate to bother you on your honeymoon! Could I borrow six bucks to get some beer?" I gladly handed him the six bucks and he went merrily on his way.

The next morning, we packed up and continued our journey north to LaLa land in Kansas. We made it home that early afternoon. It seemed that nothing had changed much except that we had a legal document showing that we were legally married.

CHAPTER 14

Moving Forward

Pam continued helping customers as they would stop in. I continued my work on the repairs that were brought into the shop and sales as well. It really troubled me that Pam continued to seek out and use illegal drugs along with her alcohol and cigarettes. I thought that maybe giving birth to a baby and new responsibilities would help her change her ways. How naive of me!

In June, Pam started having false labor quite frequently. Many times, I took her to the emergency room thinking this was it but it was on June 22 of the year that we had gotten married. This time it was for real. She was in labor dilated to the max. She came up with the name Audie while in the labor room. I was present, holding her hand the entire duration until he was born. He weighed in at 10 lbs 9 oz. It was an unforgettable experience for me.

Everything seemed to move along pretty good for a while, I assumed. I had a pretty good business built up.

Audie was just a few months old and Pam had a wicker bassinet of which she would carry him from place to place.

Towards the end of the summer that Audie was born, Pam, Rachel and I thought that we would take a trip to Phoenix, Arizona to visit Rachel's half sister on our way to California

We were heading to Disneyland, Universal Studio and Knotts Berry Farm to have a fun adventure..

After our short visit with Rachel's sister and her husband in Phoenix, we headed onward to California. Pam thought it would be nice to go out of our way to visit the Grand Canyon. I wanted to see it also, so the Grand Canyon it was! Upon our arrival, I parked my van in the parking area. No sooner than I parked, Pam threw the bassinet and baby Audie down in the back of the van! She then took off running and screaming, saying, " I hate this baby!" She was running to the Canyon just about the time she started to jump, I grabbed her by the arm as Rachell pushed her towards me. I Picked her up and threw her over my shoulder, carrying her back into the van. At that point, we exited the park not really getting to see much of the canyon at all. We then continued our trip to Las Angeles, Calif. because her relatives who lived there were expecting us.

We arrived in LA with no incidences thank God! The next day, we went to DisneyLand and Universal Studio which was a good time. The following day, as we drove up to Knotts Berry Farm, Pam started one of her tantrums again as we were parking in the parking lot. She started crying, saying I hate this baby as she threw Audie while was in the bassinet to the back of the van. Rachel caught Audie as he was falling out of the bassinet. Pam took off running out of the van into the parking lot crying and screaming. I retrieved her back into the van. After she had cooled off, we all went into the Knotts Berry Park without any further incidents .

All in all, the trip was worth what all we went through. We really enjoyed all the amusement parks for sure. Now we were ready for the daily grind of attending to getting down to business back at my store.

Not long after we got back from California, I had sold enough vacuums to be promoted to a factory distributor. I was invited to a sales meeting in New Orleans. This was a weekend event that should be exciting.

We stopped the first night at a motel which looked like a 4 star motel from the outside. I was really tired and sleepy and there were no other motels nearby so decided to stay the night even though the inside was not too appealing. The next morning we looked out the window at the pool and the water was green! We were sure glad we didn't take a dip in there! We hopped in the van and went the rest of the journey to New Orleans.

As we approached the outskirts of New Orleans, I told Pam, everyone here are black. Not that I was racist but was just obvious. I pulled the van into a parking lot to check the air in my front tire. I asked a gentleman where I could find Bourbon Street . He replied, "I don't know what you want to go to Bourbon Street for but I will tell you the way you were headed, they eat honkies down there !" I turned to Pam and asked, "What is a honky?" She replied, "honey, that is you!" I really never knew what a honky was until this moment.

We had a good elegant time at the banquet and my promotion activities that evening.

That night was quite the experience! I have never seen so many drunk people on one street in my entire life! People were falling out of the bars and off the sidewalks the entire night!

The next morning, we loaded up the van and headed north back to Kansas. We had gotten about fifty miles up the road when I pulled into a gas station to fill up. No sooner than the tank was full, a car load of black men in an old Cadillac pulled up and a young man with a gas can rushed up to me asking if I could give him a ride as he ran out of gas just up the road and over the hill. I told him that I was going to go inside and get my tire patched. Of course, I fibbed a little because I knew he was up to no good. Lo and behold, I was right! There was never a car out of gas anywhere to be seen over that hill! We went on our journey making it back home without incident.

One day, a couple of sales reps from Chicago stopped by my shop to introduce a new expensive vacuum cleaner to me to interest my salesmen to market their product. I was eager to look at their product for it seems that I had gotten a bad shipment of vacuums. The motors were burning out in no time. I was replacing the motors free of charge to the consumers. The factory sent the replacement motors to me at no charge but I was paying a repairman labor to install them for me. The factory reps agreed that if I signed up with their company to market their product they would hire more salespeople for my business.

They hired and trained several reps for me. We had a lead system that people would call our store to see which prize they had won. The only catch was that they were required to watch a demonstration of the vacuum before getting their prize. The prospects would call into the office and Pam would answer the phone to set the salesman's appointment.

We were getting a good response and lots of sales. I was getting pretty frustrated with Pam when sales were slowing down. One day, I walked into her office and there were three of the salesmen sitting in front of her desk. She had a tight white slacks on with her feet stretched onto the desk. Her skimpy blouse was very revealing. I scolded her saying, "No wonder sales are slow, all the salesmen are here in the office looking at your skimpy clothes!" The salesmen took the hint and went back to work.

Pam was still doing her drugs and all the other things that went with it. One Saturday night we had a lot of friends and relatives over at our house. They were all drinking beer. Audie was still in a wicker bassinet. Pam, threw another one of her fits again! For no reason at all, she left baby Audie on the porch, took off running as she was crying. She was saying, " I hate this baby, I hate this baby, I want my Mama, I'm going to my Mama!" She intended on walking 300 MI. to her mother's house. I caught up with her in my car a few blocks down the road. I picked her up as she screamed "I want my Mama!" I brought her back to the house where the others were caring for Audie. All the guests went to their homes and we proceeded to go to bed for the night.

Fast forward a few weeks. My sister's daughter and her husband, I was told from a reliable friend, was over at a drug dealer's house getting some pot during the day. My sister's daughter asked him, "Is that Alan's wife?" "Yes," he replied as he laughed. They never did give me any clue that she was cheating with the married drug dealer. I never suspected that she would or had even cheated on me.I was too naive to say the least. This guy, as you will learn in later chapters, is a man she eventually marries.

That summer, we decided to take a trip for the weekend to Colorado Springs, Colorado for a relaxing getaway. We headed out with our son, Audie, my mom and dad and also my sister, Esther. The trip was three hundred fifty miles from Liberal. We always had summer sausage,cheese and crackers to tide us over on the road. My dad asked for a cracker, I didn't think anything about there being a problem by handing him a cracker but all hell broke loose! Pam was mad as hell that I had given him one of her crackers! She started crying and kicking, screaming at the top of her lungs. I managed to pull over at a rest stop so that all of us could get out of the car and calm her down for a bit. After ten minutes or so, she did calm down so that we could enjoy the rest of our journey to the mountains. The mountain air was nice and so relaxing. We visited all of the sites we could for the short duration we were there.

The time came for us to make the trip back home to Kansas. We were all very tired from climbing up hill in most sites we visited. The rest of the trip was without incident the entire trip home.

We returned to Liberal on Sunday night and resumed our daily routine the next day as usual. I would pursue my efforts to making money and she would do her part setting appointments and such.

A few weeks later, I was to be at a sales convention in Kansas City, Mo. We took Pam's car. She was driving, baby Audie was sitting in the middle of the front in his car seat. I was in the passenger seat. We were about two hundred and fifty miles from home on the four hundred mile journey to Kansas City.

Pam was coming up pretty quick upon a flatbed truck in front of us. I thought we might hit it so I touched the steering wheel. Pam started screaming and started to open the door to jump out of the car. She was going seventy miles per hour at the time. I had to reach over Audie, as I steered the car, trying to grab hold of Pam to keep her from jumping out. Plus, I used my left foot reaching over to put it under the gas pedal to slow the car down. I did manage to get the car slowed down to a stop Pam jumped out of the car and took off running down the highway at the rear of the car,screaming. I jumped out of the car and caught up with her picking her up over my shoulder placing her in the passenger seat. I took the wheel the rest of the way to Kansas City.

I attended the meetings while Pam and Audie stayed at the hotel room. The meeting was only a couple of days long. That Sunday night, we returned home to Liberal without any misfortunes. After our long weekend journey, we were definitely tired the next Monday morning, I must say.

Because I had gotten quite a few business pointers to help my business at that meeting, I was raring to get the sales people into the office to get them pumped up for more sales.

We had been pretty busy with every day routine all that week. Baby Audie was just as cute as he could be. Everything was going fairly smooth for that week and the one that followed. It did come to a point that with a new baby, we needed to sell the Corvette and get a family car. I placed an ad in the newspaper and a matter of a few days sold the car and bought a nice Lincoln Continental for Pam to drive. She loved it because it had a moon roof and lots of room inside.

Things were rolling right along with no incidents to mention. I was working long hours and making good money with all the sales. We thought that it would be good to leave Audie with a sitter and go to Garden City to a nightclub called the Grain Bin. Pam and I loaded up my brother and his wife to come along for the 70 mi. ride..

My brother and his wife as well as Pam were drinking mixed drinks. I was always the designated driver so I only drank one beer.

Everyone was dancing to the music that was playing. I asked Pam if she wanted to dance to several songs. Each time, she declined to dance with me. All of a sudden, her male hairdresser from Liberal came to our table and asked her to dance. Waa Laa! She went right to the dance floor with him and not only to one song but to three songs without sitting down. That didn't sit well with me. When she sat down, I said,"You wouldn't dance with me once but you danced with your hairdresser three dances!"

That is all I said to make her run to the ladies room crying. She stayed in the ladies room for some time crying. My sister in law went into the restroom to retrieve her. As soon as she came out, she ran out of the club and hid behind the trash can crying, saying, "Why me? why me? I want my ma ma?"

When we approached her, she took off running and crying down the sidewalk along the highway. My brother, his wife and I got into her Lincoln. We caught up to her down the road. My brother said, " I'll get her into the car." He picked her up over his shoulder and as he did, she bit him hard! She was kicking and screaming and crying as he placed her onto the front passenger seat and quickly shut the door. Immediately she bit a chunk of leather off the interior of the door! She was screaming as she cried while kicking the dash.

My sister didn't live far from there in Garden City so that is where we headed as she was screaming and crying. As we pulled up to my sister's house, she jumped out of the car and disappeared into the darkness. We couldn't find her anywhere. I called the police to find her. Moments later, the police brought her to my sister's house. The officer told us he found her sitting on the library steps crying. She settled down as we got back into the car for our journey home without further incidence that night.

The following weekend, Pam and my two brother's wives thought that they should go dragging main while drinking beer while Pam drove. I didn't. take a liking to the fact that they had Audie with them in the car.

I caught up with them on Pancake Boulevard. As I pulled up beside them,.I yelled," Pam," you girls do what you want but let Audie come home with me." Pam replied, "Audie will be fine with us. He can just stay with us." There was nothing else I could do to persuade her so I turned around and went back home. It was pretty cold out that winter night, I went home and turned the t.v. on.

Along about midnight or so, I had gotten kind of curious as to why they were out so late. I decided to check on them. I located them at a motel bar. It was a bar where a woman was murdered, stabbed to death at the back door in an alley a couple of weeks prior. Lo and behold, they left Audie in the car asleep with the engine running in the same spot that the lady was murdered in that alley. I retrieved Audie from the back seat and brought him home with me right away! It wasn't long after this incident that she dropped her friends off and returned home.

Pam walked into the house like nothing happened as she got on the phone with her sister-in-law she had dropped off. I went right to sleep for the rest of the night.

Fast forwarding a week or two later, we went to a family penny ante poker game that they had over at a friends house. They liked Chicago high low split. Seems that we later figured out why they liked high low split and always managed to win the pot. The woman would turn her ring up if she was betting high and turn her ring down to go low. That way, they split the pot. We decided we wouldn't play that game any more with them.

Seems that the drama just kept on and on and on with Pam! She was a drama Queen! One night, about eleven o'clock, for no reason at all, she took baby Audie, loading him in the car seat in the Lincoln. She called me to say that she was going to Kansas City and was going to drive off a cliff! I immediately called the police to have her stopped. I jumped in my vehicle and proceeded to look for her. I didn't see her anywhere in town.

I drove east on highway 54 towards the edge of town and up the road a mile or so away from me, I saw some tail lights that looked like her's. I sped upon the car, sure enough, it was her and Audie! They were already out of town. I called the sheriff in the next county to have her stopped. He never located her even though I gave him the location. I then called the police in the little town of Minneola. The sheriff's deputy stopped her at the convenience store fortunately.

I told him that she had told me she was going to drive off a cliff. After he talked to her for awhile, he came to me and told me that she has some very serious mental issues that need attention. I asked him to please let me put. Audie in the car with me. Pam agreed, so I headed back on the sixty mile or so journey home with Audie and Pam followed in her car. When we reached home, it was the wee hours of the night and we called it another usual,normal day around our home. We all went right to sleep in no time.

Fast forward Christmas, Christmas was the most important day of the entire year for Pam's mom. Her mom would shop for the next year's Christmas the next day after Christmas and during the entire year. Because that Holliday was so important to her and her mom, I closed my shop for almost an entire week to celebrate with them. A person would not believe all the presents Pam's little spoiled brother had to open. He had like thirty presents, nice presents! As he opened one after another, he would not even smile or act excited. I could not believe he never said a thank you!

I never felt very comfortable at their large home that used to be an old Colonial type nursing home. Pam and I would occupy her old bedroom at our stay up stairs. Pam did not want her mom to know that she smoked cigarettes so she would curl up in the corner on the floor between the nightstand and wall sneaking a smoke.

We were at the end of our stay there and I felt that after having my shop closed for business, we needed to get back the next morning on that three hundred mile journey.

The night before the planned trip home, Pam was down stairs on the couch with her mom and I was sitting on the steps to the upstairs. It was one a.m. in the morning so I was tired and sleepy to say the least.

I politely said to Pam, "Are you ready to go to bed, we have a long trip back home tomorrow?" Pam's mother came unglued! She pops up from the couch saying, " What gives you the right to have an orgee (as she spoke it) in your mother in law's house? No one is allowed to have an orgee in my house!" I abruptly replied, " I'll have an orgee (as she put it) anywhere, anytime I want and it's no one's damn business!" Nothing was even spoken about sex in the first place. I felt that this was all uncalled for to say the least!

The next morning we loaded up the van and said our goodbyes before our journey back home. I never liked my mother in law very much after the way she showed me so much disrespect though! I really believe it was due to all the lies that Pam was feeding her about me.

CHAPTER 15

Conquest for Rachel

As the weeks went by, I became more and more concerned about Rachel's well being in Amarillo, Texas. I was receiving concerns that she was being left alone with drunk men who were strangers to her while she would go out partying at the bars.

I had no choice but to file change of residential custody in the Seward County District Court in Liberal, Ks.

Little did I know that I would have to go through the process of having to hire seven separate attorneys as I afore. mentioned, her dad was a practicing attorney and would make it as difficult as possible for me to succeed.

I had a struggle finding an attorney who could help with the representation I needed to gain change of residential custody of Rachel. After having had to hire so many different attorneys, one of the ladies in the district court office took me to the side and recommended a good attorney for. He was more costly but would be able to get the job done. Kelly fought as hard as she could but my high dollar attorney did his job well. Rachel was able to live with me and Pam as her custodial parents in Kansas.

Pam was none too happy that Rachel was to live with us. She felt that I was giving Rachel more attention than her most of the time. She was not very good at playing the part as a stepmom to say the least !

Pam became pregnant again before we obtained custody of Rachel. She became very adamant for us to purchase a two story house in the middle of town area. She was really interested in the one that was three blocks from the married man's home of whom I would later learn that she was having an affair with. I didn't have a clue that she was having an affair with anyons at this time at all . She begged me to buy this particular house. I personally didn't like it. It was priced too high and not so nice. She promised me that she would treat me like a King if I would buy that house. Her plea was to no avail, I would have to keep shopping for another one. Pam was being pretty direct and impatient about getting a two story house.

Fast forwarding a few more weeks, Pam started her fits again. She just couldn't get used to Rachel. I did not know about this at the time it happened, I was at work but she took her out back and beat her with a belt buckle all over her body, including her head because she didn't bring her homework home. Rachel told me that Pam would have her thoroughly clean the house every day. She said if Pam would see one pan not put away, she would throw a glass full of ice with the water at her face while she was sleeping. I never knew of this at the time as well.

Later Pam packed a few things, loaded up Audie and her things into the Lincoln, all the while, she was crying! She would drive off not saying where she was going. She never came home all that night. I had no idea where her and Audie may have gone. I did, though figure she would make the 300 mi. trip to her mom's.

I called her mom's house several times for the next three days but her mom would just hang up the phone on me. I lost my cool so I ventilated and went to a local car dealer and bought a nice sports car to replace my Corvette. As I mentioned, I had sold it to buy her the Lincoln Continental. The very next day,she and Audie showed up back home in Liberal as if nothing had happened. .

I did find a two story house for sale that was priced right in the middle of town. I signed a contract to purchase the home for Pam . Pam, Rachel, little Audie and I were satisfied that the house would suffice for all of us.

It wasn't long that we were moved into the house. It was quite roomy and well arranged. Everyone had their own room. I used to tell Audie bedtime stories and read to him out of a children's book. He really loved it! He enjoyed my funny version of 'The three Bears' and "Little Red Riding Hood' I would make the stories more comical for him. He would cuddle up and fall right to sleep.

Our new house was just a couple of blocks from a church preschool called Rainbow school that we had enrolled him in. He really enjoyed going to school. I would walk him there every morning. He was so cute! Every time we would drive by the school, Audie would point out "Here is Audie's Rainbow school."

Pam was still being difficult to put up with. She many times would still go into the bedroom for no reason, slam the door, crying as she would say, " Why me? Why me? Waaaaaaaa waaaaaa! I want my Mama!" Waaaaaaa! As usual, I would go buy her either some roses or her favorite of all, a unicorn trinket.

Pam was in her third trimester of her second pregnancy. She did not like the idea of being pregnant for a minute. One morning, Pam was at the kitchen stove cooking breakfast. I was sitting at the kitchen table with Rachel over in the corner across the room. I asked Pam very politely, "Could you throw Rachel a couple of eggs on the skillet too? " Pam came unglued! She reached her hand into the garbage disposal, grabbing garbage and throwing it at Rachel as she screamed profanity at her. She next proceeded to place her own entire head in the sink of dirty dish water trying to drown herself. I grabbed her by her hair retrieving her head out of the sink so that she wouldn't drown.

Next, she grabbed a handful of her valium and stuck them into her mouth. I pressed her cheeks really hard so that they would exit her mouth. It didn't end there! Believe it or not, she grabbed a long butcher knife, as she was saying, " I hate this baby ! I hate this baby!" She then tried to stab her stomach! I managed to free the knife from her tightly clenched fist. She ran up to the bedroom saying, "Why me? Why me? I want my ma ma! and continue crying for what seemed like forever! Crying and wanting her mother as usual, I would, like a dummy, go fetch her more flowers at the grocery store or some trinket that she adored to quieten her down once more.

Poor Rachel, I know that I was naive and a fool for not notifying the authorities about the going ons that occurred almost daily in our home! It wasn't only things that she did to Rachel but on another occasion, Pam was talking to her mother. I picked up the extension phone because I knew they would be running me down, talking bad about me. To my surprise, her mother told Pam that she knew a mafia doctor that she could obtain some pills to bring her from her home 300 miles away to abort the baby she was carrying. Pam told her to please see about getting them and bring them to her at our home.

A few days later, I had noticed a car in town that looked to be her mother's which had a licence plate from the county she was from. I immediately drove home to confront Pam as to why her mom would be in town. I said to her, " I see that your mother is in town. Did she bring you those pills to kill our baby?" " I do not want her in this house and you had better not take those Damn pills!" She starting crying and yelling at me so I turned around, exiting the house to my van. I drove off and went for a short drive to cool off from being so angry. When I drove up from my 15 minute exit, as soon as I entered the house, she approached me very angrily, slapping my face as hard as she could as she said to me, " I wasn't done talking to you. Don't you leave like that while I'm talking!" I again demanded that if her mom brought any pills to her, she had better not take them ! I do not know to this day if she did or did not . I do know that the baby wasn't aborted. Thank God! Pam's mother didn't stay in town for long and returned home that night without ever seeing much of me that day.

The drama around our new home was non stop! Pam was relentlessly abusive to Rachel so much that I came home one evening from work asking where she was. Pam told me that she had had enough of Rachel not doing the chores as instructed. I proceeded to look for Rachel around the house. I opened the front room closet and there was thirteen year old Rachel on the floor with a belt tightly around her neck, trying to commit suicide! I took her out of the dark closet and brought her over to my mother's house to stay with her until we could work things out. It was heartbreaking to see this. I should have sought help of some kind for my crazy wife but I was too dumb or naive to do so.

A week or so later, I went to my mother's to bring Rachel back home . Pam was having false labor with the baby pretty frequently. Many times I had to take her to the emergency room to see what was occurring . Finally, the time came that it was not false labor. I took her to Garden City hospital for delivery because she was wanting a spinal tap so as not to feel the pain. I went to the delivery room with her as I did the same with Audie to welcome them into this world. This is when my second daughter was born weighing in at 6 lbs. 4 oz. We will call her Marilyn. What a joy!

The following day, we brought Marylin home in her wicker bassinet into our bedroom for a peaceful nap. Marylin was such a sweet,cute little baby!

Having little Marylin didn't slow Pam's

episodes hardly at all. A person would think that she would be a much happier person after having a new born baby girl!

One day, Pam ordered as usual for Rachel to go to work deep cleaning the house. Rachel. still at the age of thirteen was more than willing to do the task. Pam filled Rachel a big glass bowl of hot Lysol water for her to clean with. Pam was going to the store or somewhere at the time. She handed Rachel the bowl and a brush instructing her to scrub the kitchen walls, then to clean the front room walls while Pam stepped out .

Lo and Behold! Rachel cleaned the front room first rather than the kitchen first as she was told! Pam walked in, she saw that Rachel was doing the front room first. Pam was hysterical! She started crying and yelling at Rachel for not following her orders . Pam then demanded that she leave the house and not return! As Rachel was leaving out the front door, BAMM! Pam threw the glass bowl of Lysol water at her. Rachel ducked and the bowl hit the corner of the door. I was not home at the time, I was working out of town. I never knew about the many times that Pam awakened Rachel from sleep . She would pour a glass of ice water onto her face because she had noticed a dish or something that Rachel had forgotten to put away into the cabinet when she would do the dishes. It was never revealed to me until some time later.

Because of the drama at our home, Rachel went to her cousin's house who was her same age. They were very close to each other. Again, I should have contacted the authorities to report this abuse! By not having contacted the proper authorities, I had greatly hindered a good future for not only myself but much worse, for Audie and Marylin! You will learn in the remaining chapters that with no legal documentation, it is next to impossible to have anyone believe your story as told by yourself or either of the children.

CHAPTER 16

The Last Straw

Fast forwarding a month or so. Rachel seemed to be pretty happy and content over at her cousin's two story house. She was sharing the same bedroom without being yelled at by Pam.

During this time, Pam and my relationship was a nightmare! Pam was getting out of control. She enrolled into our local college and had made a lot of friends to hang out with. Pam would bad mouth me to all of her friends . She would even say things to her entire class as to how possessive her husband was of her. What she wasn't telling them was, the only things I was possessive about in her eyes was her use of illegal drugs and her skimpy, revealing attire.

Pam had more friends to use her drugs with now that she was going to school. There were a couple of single guys next door who would come to the down stairs bathroom window to offer her some drugs called ice. Our upstairs bathroom facing their apartment had a large window. At night, she would leave the blinds open for viewing with the light on as she would undress for them, I was told.

Pam covered all the bases as far as to make me look bad to anyone she came into contact with, unfortunately. I heard her tell her mom as she was talking on the phone that she thought I was the kind of retarded person of sorts that you can't tell is retarded. What Ever! Considering the source !

Rachel continued to stay with her cousin and a lot of time with my mother. I was really torn emotionally about these circumstances. I was sure that Rachel felt unjustly rejected. Rachel and I have always been close our entire lives. It was not right that we should have had to live our lives that way because of a crazy woman!

I still had my shop down town that was taking in business. I would go out drumming up business while my office girl would take care of the customers who would come into our store. The girl told me that Pam would come into the shop taking a fist full of cash ! She told her, "Don't tell Alan I took this." She obviously was using the money to support her drug habit. I paid all of the bills and bought all of her cigarettes and everything else for her. It was pretty rude and disrespectful for her to put my employee in such a situation to say the least!

I was getting more and more suspicious of Pam's activities. A few times, I would see her suspected boyfriend in the next block laying back on the seat of his Harley as to be waiting for someone. Many times, I would see him drive by our house in his car. She would hang out with some people with little character frequently that really was a concern to me.

She wore skimpy, revealing clothes that revealed more than a person would need to see. The neighbor across the street told me that she has seen Pam answer the door with nothing but a shirt on. She told me that she would have to get onto her husband for goo goo eying over towards my house as Pam would sit on the front steps doing her homework in a short skirt with no panties on. The neighbor lady also informed me that many times, she would see me leave for work. She told me that as I would exit out the back door and down the alley, two African American neighbor men from next door would come inside the front door with my wife. This was just getting to be way more than I had bargained to deal with.

Our relationship was hanging by a string. It was sad, Rachel was not with me. I had a wife that was loose and suspected of having an affair! What was worse, she was bragging to my sister-in-law that she put wine in Marylin's baby bottle saying it put her right to sleep. This was really not a good marriage whatsoever!

As I mentioned in an earlier chapter, I had a business downtown. One day, pretty close to closing time for my shop, a friend of my wife's suspected boyfriend' stopped by to delay me from going home. He wanted to show me his Cadillac. He was really taking his sweet time pointing out every detail on his car. I didn't even know the man that well to say the least. Before I left the office to head home, I received a call from the city inspector who happened to be friends with her suspected boyfriend also. The inspector asked me to come by his house for a bit to talk to me about my permit I received to have a business sign installed in front of my shop.

Instead of going home as intended, I stopped at the innovator's home who lived across the street a few houses down from mine. When he opened the door, he invited me to sit down . As I sat, another man who was with him was across the room from me. I thought it was peculiar how the two of them were giggling to each other and the inspector had gotten onto his phone briefly mumbling to the party on the other end. He never talked to me about the permit or the sign in the least!

After twenty or so minutes, I headed to my house which was only a block away. As I was pulling up the long driveway, I noticed a pickup parked across the way. It looked to be that of Herman's, who I suspected Pam of seeing! I immediately reached for my phone and called his wife. I asked her, "Does your husband drive a green ford pickup?" She immediately started crying and went on to say, " Oh no! He is seeing your wife ? She is so beautiful! Boo hoo hoo. " Obviously he was! At that point, I hung my phone up not knowing what else to say.

There was no more guessing about the standing of our marriage. I didn't say anything to Pam about it at all. I knew she would deny even knowing this guy. Besides, our wedding anniversary was coming up in the next few days.

Our anniversary didn't mean anything to Pam obviously! The next day or two, after she had been on the phone with her mom quite often, she loaded Audie and Marylin into the car and headed to her mom's house up state. She hardly said a word, she sobbed as she loaded her things into the car and drove off without saying when she would return home.

I would call her mom's house. Her mom would answer the phone each time. Everytime I asked to speak to Pam, her mom would hang the phone up . It had gotten to be the day before our wedding anniversary when I called one last time. This time Pam answered the phone. I asked Pam, " Pam, when are you and the kids coming home?" Pam said to me, " I don't know." I then told her that if she wasn't home by our anniversary, I would talk to an attorney about a divorce.

I decided I would make the 300 mile drive up to Pam's mom and dad's house to talk to her and to see the kids. I drove up to their house noticing that Pam's car was on the property. I exited my Firebird car and commenced to knock on their door.

Pam's mom answered the door as she abruptly sprung the door open. She was rude as she gave me a glaring look. She exclaimed, " Pam is not here!" From behind her comes running to me, jumping into my arms was 3 year old Audie.

I, with Audie in my arms, rushed to my car, sitting Audie into his car seat. Pam's mom was right on my tail. As I was locking Audie in his seat, she grabbed the key from the ignition. I asked her for as I sat in the driver's seat. She told me that she would give me the key when I handed Audie over to her. I felt I had no choice as she walked back into her house slamming the door! After 5 or 10 minutes, I realized that I was wasting my time, besides, it was very hot that day with no key to start the air conditioner in the car.

I carried Audie as he wrapped his arms around my neck and crying as I carried him to the house to surrender him in exchange for the keys to the car .

I called Pam's mom on the phone and asked when Pam would return. She told me that Pam left with some friends in the next town not telling her when she would return.

I decided to go back Home without even talking to Pam. I was feeling empty and helpless. I made the 5 hour journey home to decide my next move. When I arrived at my home, it felt very lonely and quiet. I slept on the couch feeling very sad and depressed, lying there thinking as what to do.

The next day, which was our anniversary, I waited for her return home. She did not call or answer any of my calls that day whatsoever! This was the last straw!

CHAPTER 17

The Divorce from Hell

had finally figured that I would have to do what I needed to do without fail. I set an appointment with an attorney to file for divorce. I really made a very bad choice of an attorney though. I chose an attorney who was best friends with the judge. I did make a wrong decision regretfully! You will learn in this chapter that just because an attorney and judge frequent the bars together most nights could really work against your welfare in more ways than one for your case!

No sooner than I signed the papers for the divorce, I received a call from my attorney ! He says, " hello Alan, how are you?" I replied, "Ok, how are you doing?" He says, "I am talking to your wife's attorney right now on the other line" I replied, "WHAT?" He explained to me that she had hired her an attorney as soon as she had gotten back into town. I had filed for divorce only moments before she did! She had gotten one of the most experienced, highest dollar attorneys in this part of the country! You always get what you pay for in most cases.

Her request of the court was asking that she be awarded full custody of Audie and Marilyn. She was also asking the court to allow me one day a month supervised visitation! This is the woman who had tried to abort and stab both of these children while in her womb with a butcher knife telling me how she would fight tooth and nail for her children!

I asked the court that I would have temporary custody of Audie only because Marilyn was still breastfeeding. I felt that Pam should have temporary custody of Marilyn for that reason. I also was temporarily awarded the right to live in our two story house with Audie and Rachel while the divorce was being pursued.

A good friend of Pam's who was in good with the management of a low income apartment complex had gotten her into an apartment that she would be able to move into very soon. Because she would have no furniture, I suggested that I would stay at my mother's house along with Audie and Rachel. Pam and Marilyn could stay in the house until she could move into her new apartment.

The divorce papers stated that the household goods would be divided equally between the two of us. They also stated that I would have possession of the wicker furniture as well as half of the other furniture and supplies.

Pam's mom, one of my friends I had flown to Chicago with for our insurance licensing training while back along with his daughter were all helping her move out of the house.

After a few days of all of all the moving, I was getting concerned about what was taking so long. I called Pam and asked her, " Pam, what the hell are you doing? Are you cleaning the house out ?" Pam replied, " I am being plenty fair, we have not been in a rush." I then figured I would just wait and see what was divided after she had completed moving out.

Finally, the last day of their moving, as I drove up into the long driveway, I noticed my mother in law's pickup was loaded down with the damn railroad ties that were along the driveway ! This did not set well with me to say the least ! It was more the principle of it all. She gave her mom my railroad ties to her mom to take home with her up north. Because I did not like even being in the same room with her mother, I waited for Pam and her mom to leave with this very last load before I would even go into the house to check things out.

Pam gave me a call about an hour or so later stating that she had finished moving out. I then made my way to the house to see what she had left for Audie, Rachel and I. As I opened the front door, I could not believe my eyes ! She had taken everything out of the house other than Audie and my clothes, Audie's bed, dresser, a three legged table and a dead hanging plant! Yes, she was fair alright ! She took all the dishes, bedding, towels and anything she could get her hands on.

Pam and Marilyn were settled in their apartment. Audie, Rachel and I had our big house with very little furnishings. I contacted my attorney to remedy the situation. The best that happened was she contacted me saying that she would leave the excess household furnishings for me to pick up off of her porch. I went over to her apartment to pick them up the day I was notified to do so. It was really of no surprise to me to see two cardboard boxes full of old dishes and miscellaneous items of no value.

A friend of hers told me that she had seen Pam crying her eyes out. Her friend thought that she was crying because she didn't have Audie. Pam told her that she was upset because she ordered by the court to give up the wicker furniture to be in my possession. She never did turn loose of the wicker, ever! I just let her keep it for it wasn't worth the drama!

CHAPTER 18

Conflict of Interest

N ow that the divorce had been filed, we were notified by the court that a person of the domestic services dept. of the court would be in charge of investigating our background and circumstances. She would be the most powerful authority in recommending which of the two parents the children would reside.

Just days after the notification of the domestic investigation, I received a call at my office from the court services officer. She introduced herself over the phone. Her name of whom I shall refer to as Ms Tommie .

Ms Tommie, After a brief introduction, said, "Alan, could you please come over to my office for a few minutes? I have a couple of questions for you?" I replied that I would be right there for it was just a couple of blocks from my shop. I immediately placed a note on my shop door stating that I would return in 30 minutes.

When I arrived, Ms Tommie shook my hand and introduced herself again. Ms Tommie was an African American lady, she was about 5 ft 5 in and probably weighed 200 pounds. She was very proud of her job I could conclude.

She told me to have a seat. This I did as I noticed she had an unflattering look on her face towards me. She said, " Alan ! My job is to investigate you and Pam's lives to decide the future of your two children and who they would be best suited to live with. I, at the conclusion of my investigation, will make my recommendation in a report to the court as to who should have custody."

Ms Tommie then said to me, "Alan, Sherry and I are best friends, why did you call her and tell her that Herman was having an affair with your wife? That was very cruel of you! You hurt her very badly, she could hardly stop crying! You don't care who you hurt!" I replied to her that all I did was to call her to ask if Herman hm drove a green ford pickup. When she told me he did, all I said was that one parked in the next street. Sherry then started crying so I hung the phone up at that point.' Ms Tommie had no more questions for me at this time but told me she would be back in touch with me soon.

The next day, I called my attorney reporting to him about the investigator being friends with Sherry. He didn't see a problem with it at all. At that point, I should have fired him right then and there! When I told my attorney that Pam was pretty promiscuous, he replied, "I don't know how she missed the judge and I " Remarks such as that made me wonder what I have gotten into.

The problem was that I had already given this attorney a retainer. Being that he and the judge were always together at the bars as good friends, may have had far worse consequences if I had fired him though.

To make matters worse, my income had been reduced substantially due to all of the drama. I had not been producing sales and regular business dealings as I normally would have done. I would have no chance of winning custody with a laid back, low energy attorney up against Pam's high dollar aggressive attorney. Not a chance!

Ms Tommie called me just about every day at my shop to have me come over to her office to ask me more questions. It was really very stressful and obnoxious to say the least !

Ms Tommie even told me on one of our meetings that because of my big mouth, I was hurting Herman's financial dealings by mentioning drug use. She told me that he and my wife may have to move to either Texas or Alaska to start a new life. Herman would do so by putting in for a transfer with his employer's company. I knew that it would be devastating for our visitation possibilities if that were to come to pass!

My financial situation had gotten so bad that I could hardly pay all the bills and car payments on three cars. I was rather annoyed one day when Herman drove by my shop in the new car I was making payments on for Pam. What really took the cake was that he gave me the middle finger as he sped by with a laughing grin! I was to the point where I had no choice other than to declare bankruptcy. because of the dramatic loss of income. I did so within the next few weeks. Pam was putting the word out for folks not to do business with me plus all the far out accusations she was making about me to top it off.

Our separation was too dramatic to deal with at times. One morning I went for breakfast at a restaurant that I frequented regularly. This restaurant was run by a friend of Pam's. As I was finishing my breakfast, I asked the waitress for a refill on my coffee. She reluctantly refilled my cup after quite a wait. The next day or so, I happened to run across the waitress in the mall. She told me that Pam's friend said to her that if she would pour me another cup of coffee, she would fire her. She said that I was a paranoid schizophrenic! That was really something said coming from a woman as unstable as Pam!

Ms Tommie was really obnoxious, always harassing me to come to her office to talk to her rather than to just ask me her questions that could be answered over the phone.

One afternoon, Ms Tommie called me, she asked me to come over to her office again. As I entered her office, she says to me, " Have a seat Alan. Alan, I have done an extensive investigation of you and Pam. I went doe to doe (door) talking to people. I have learned that Pam could be a nurse by day and a prostitute by night! But Richard, I haven't been able to find out anything about you at all yet! Everyone has a skeleton in their closet and I know you have a skeleton out there somewhere! I am going to find it !" I had no more to say to her other than that I needed to get back to work and thanked her for her time.

It was quite a dramatic experience it seemed most of the time. Seems that Herman was pretty upset with me for listing the new car of Pam's on the bankruptcy. Everytime I would see the guy, he would flip me the bird. It was hard to take but I just did the best I could to ignore him.

The custody investigation was so extensive. Ms Tommie was going door to door asking questions from any known drug users. She accused me of following her around as she was doing so.

A concerned relative of mine who was good friends with shady persons warned me that a gang had taken a vote as to whether to put a hit on me or not. He said that the vote was yes. I told him that I would not back down, not for a minute. As the readers of this novel will learn in another chapter, the widow of the hitman from Chicago told my son that her husband was paid to kill me by my wife's boyfriend. Fortunately, for me the hit man was shot in the head and thus killed before that ever happened.

A week or so later, Ms Tommie gave me another call. She asked me to come over to her office again. While I was there, Sherry had called her. Ms Tommie told her that they should go to the sonic for lunch at noon. I then told her about the neighbor lady telling me about the times that when I left for work exiting out the back door, the two men came into the house through the front door.

She then said to me, "I know what two black men would do with one white woman ! Let's get in my car and you show me where they live.'" We got into her car to head in the direction of their house, then, all of a sudden, she flipped a u turn heading back to her office! I didn't know what to think about that ordeal to say the least. When we arrived at her office, I had no idea as to why she acted the way she did. I got into my van and went back to work.

The custody Investigation went on for months and months. My niece,during this time, just happened to move right next door in an apartment to Pam! One Sunday afternoon, my neice's mom, Esther, called me and asked if I would bring my mother over to visit for a while. My mother and I went on over to my niece's for a visit with my sister, Esther.

After a short while, Audie came over from his mom's from next door to see my sister, my mom and I. The problem was that Pam had Audie staying at her home for her weekend visitation. Audie wasn't there for anytime at all when there was someone pounding on the door. To our surprise it was Ms Tommie! She said, " Alan! You and your mother leave right now! She said, "You just go on home now! I was just this close (holding two fingers an inch apart) to giving you custody. Now that I see how you would be if you had custody, I am not going to recommend that you do! Now get on home, and Audie, you get back over to your mother's house!" Needless to say, my mother and I went back to our homes without saying a word. We just could not believe what we just heard.

The following week, my attorney called me into his office. He explained to me that Ms. Tommie had finished her report and recommended that the court award custody of the children to their mother. He told me that because my mother and I going over to visit my sister and niece while Pam had Audie at her apartment was the straw that broke the camel's back! If I hadn't answered the phone call from by sister that day, I may have been awarded custody!

My attorney told me that 99% of the time, the court abides by the court services officer's recommendations. I had informed my attorney and Ms Tommie of the officer's name in Minneola, Kansas who talked to Pam in the wee hours of the morning when she was on her way to drive herself and Audie off the cliff. My attorney told me that the officer did not remember the incident happening. I asked that my sister's in laws be asked about leaving baby Audie in the running car in the cold behind the bar parked in the alley where a woman was murdered weeks previously while they were inside the bar. They were not subpoenaed either. I asked him about the times that she tried to kill herself with a butcher knife while pregnant with both babies . No-one would believe Rachel or l. I asked him about the time she tried to jump into the Grand Canyon, again, the only witnesses were Rachel and I. My attorney should have filed a motion to have Ms Tommie removed from this case long before it came thus far due to a conflict of interest.

I hardly ever cry except for maybe when a death of a loved one comes about but I did have tears in my eyes along with Audie the night we had gotten the word of Ms. Tommie's recommendation that gloomy day !

CHAPTER 19

The Pursuit for Justice Round 2

Our nasty divorce was finally finalized but the battle still was to continue over the years for the welfare of Audie and Marylin.

The court, although Pam was asking that I should have one day a week supervised visitation, I was awarded every other weekend and alternating holidays and 60 days summer visitations. I was asking for the entire summer but the best I could have gotten was the 60 days. She wanted it 60 days because some months have 31 days in them.

No sooner than we had gotten out the gate, Pam took Audie and Marylin to her mom's and would not bring them to Liberal for our weekend visitation. Her family ignored my phone calls and would not allow me any contact with the children. I had to pay another attorney to enforce the court ordered visitation!

The next day or so, Pam's mother did bring the children back to town for our visitation after having been served. They didn't like the idea of having to conform to the court's order to say the least.

Fast forwarding a month or so, I was sitting in my van in a parking lot late at night messing with my stereo. I heard a knock on the passenger side window when I noticed as I looked up, Herman with his nose smashed against the window giving me the middle finger ! I stepped outside of my van to confront him but he was already about a hundred feet away by a building. I then told him that I thought that he did me a favor running off with my wife but I was really pissed off about my kids! He just laughed out loud as he walked away. I then got back into my van and went on my way.

Soon after the incident with Herman, Rachel's sister who lived in Phoenix invited her and I there for a visit, Rachel and her sister had talked about Rachel attending the school year there in Phoenix. It was towards the end of July and school would begin very soon. I booked a flight to Phoenix for our one week visit. The visit was very relaxing, although it was so hot there. Seems we spent most days in Rachel's sister's swimming pool more than anything else.

The week went by pretty fast and I was ready to get back home where it wasn't so howas too Rachel to ths school there to get her registered. At the last moment, she started crying, telling me that she wanted to go back home with me.

I told Rachel that she could come back with me to Kansas. The next day, we boarded the plane back home. We arrived in Liberal on Sunday evening, upon our arrival, as we left the airport in Liberal, we swung down the road past Pam's apartment, not stopping but just to drive by. As we did. I noticed that the curtains were taken down and it looked as though she had moved. I talked to a neighbor down the street who told me that Audie had told her son that he was moving and he was not supposed to tell anyone.

Because it was stipulated in the divorce that we both had joint custody, neither party was to move out of the state without notifying the court of such intentions. She had moved somewhere without a word to the court of her intentions!

I was lost for words,. I was not only lost for words but very angry. I called around to different ones who might have known where she may have moved off to but no-one seemed to know anything. I contacted my attorney but he wasn't too concerned about it .

I had noticed that Herman had recently sold his house that he and his wife had lived in. The next day, I contacted a realtor friend of mine to see if he could find out as to where Pam and Herman had moved our children to and maybe I could make contact with her. My friend told me that they had moved to Beaumont, Texas, that's about seven hundred miles away. He also gave me their phone number at their house.

I called the number from another phone other than my own the number that he had given me. The lady who answered the phone was Pam trying to talk with a Mexican accent to throw me off. When she answered the phone, I called her Pam. She told me that she was the cleaning lady and Pam and Herman were not home. I said to her that I knew that she was Pam and I was going to file for custody modification at the courthouse.

So hear we go again! I had to hire another attorney to file for modification of custody. I chose to file a motion for a change of custody instead because of her actions.

There would have to be another home study and an evaluation to be done with a mental health professional and all of that that goes with the process.

Another court services officer was appointed this time to do the home study investigation. Ms. Tommie was no longer employed with the court .

The very first thing, Pam and Herman had driven right on up to Liberal to talk to the new court services officer Jennie to put her two cents in with her. Come to find out later, I was told that Pam had gone to school with this lady !

We were under court orders to get a psychological evaluation both for ourselves and the children. There were also home studies ordered on both sides.

Marylin and Audie were revealing to the professional therapist a few concerning events happening at their home in Texas.

They both were complaining that there were illegal drugs being used Pam and Herman and also about being beaten with a belt when they would tell Pam or Herman that they wanted to live with me. They told of times being locked out of the house in 100 degree temperatures. Marylin complained that she had to take baths with Herman also. Audie told about when he had asked where babies came from, Herman did the unthinkable. Herman pulled Marylin's panties down, spread her legs to show Audie. Herman replied," This is where babies come from!" Audie told me that it made him sick to his stomach.

Audie and Marylin told me that when the children's protective services officer showed up at their home in Texas, Pam told them that they had a whisper 2000 and would be listening to everything they would tell the lady. Audie and Marylin were frightened to say about anything at all.

On our way back to Liberal with Audie and Marylin after picking them up in Dallas, Audie said, "Daddy, there is something I need to tell you, it is important!" Audie told me that after picking up his mom from her work as a nurse at the hospital, told Herman that she had left her pot in her locke, so Herman flipped a u and brought her back to retrieve it from her locker.

When we got back to Kansas, I brought Audie with me to my Attorney's office. He told my attorney about the abuses and the drugs. My attorney immediately advised me to have Audie, who was in the second grade at the time to collect some of the drugs. He told Audie to call the police and give it to them when he returned to Texas after the visit with me in Kansas.

After talking to my attorney, a few days later, as the kids and I were driving by the sheriff's office, Audie saw a deputy getting out of his car. He exclaimed that he wanted to talk to him and see if he could help him and Marylin who was 8 at the time. I parked the car next to the deputy when all three of us approached the officer. I told the deputy that the children wanted to file a police report.

We went on into his office and sit down at the table. The officer handed Audie who was twelve at the time a police report from to fill out. Out of the blue, Marylin says, " I want to fill one out too." The officer handed little Marylin a form to fill out also. When completed the officer took the top copy to file the report and handed me the carbon copies. The children both wrote the complaints that corresponded to each other's report. Be mindful that neither one spoke to each other as to compare notes.

At the end of our allotted visitation, I flew Audie and Marylin back to their home. After their return home, Audie took my attorney's advice and collected the pot to hide in his clubhouse. Audie called the police to give it to them. They arrested Pam for possession but she had gotten it dropped to disorderly conduct, serving no jail time and was fined $500.

I had contacted Audie's teacher who had told me that she was very concerned about abuse and the fact that Audie was having to take care of his little sister most of the time by themselves until their parents get home from work. I had her provide an affidavit to that fact to my attorney for the judge with no problem.

At the completion of the investigation, the mental health professional in Kansas comprised a report concluding that it would be dangerous for the children to remain in Texas with their mom and step dad.

Weeks later, upon the conclusion of the court hearing, the judge denied my request to grant a change of residential custody. He ordered that the children remain with their mom. The children reluctantly left back to Texas with Pam and Herman that was a sad, sad day for the children and me as well.

Not much time had gone by that there was an article in the local newspaper that the judge who handled our case was charged with indecent liberties with a minor. That was quite interesting.

CHAPTER 20

Pursuit for Justice Round Three

went back to the normal grind of things the best I could for the next year. The children would beg me to get them away from drugs and the abuse. Almost every time I talked to them on our weekly call, they would say, "Please, Daddy, get us out of here!" Then he would proceed to inform me of any and all occurrences that may have happened there.

I was fed up with the continuing mental and physical abuses. As time moved on, I had gotten more concerned with reports of continued use of illegal drugs and and all of the other abuses.

The kids told me that they were instructed to call Herman Dad and were made to call me by my first name. They were continually beaten with a belt if they mentioned that they wanted to live with me. Audie was made to clean up kitten poop that had maggots on it with his bare hands he had told me! I was none too happy to hear that the expensive gifts I had bought for them would always be made fun of by Herman or would mysteriously disappear.

Audie also told me of times that Herman had told him that he was embarrassed of Audie as he watched him play softball. He told him that he ran like a girl. That is no way to build the self esteem of a young boy! Marylin was always reporting to me that Herman would make fun of her singing whenever she sung. It just always broke my heart to hear all of these things that had such a negative influence on the children's self confidence.

Another Spring break came along and I picked the children up in Amarillo,Texas at the airport. The children and I made the trip to Denver, Colorado to stay for spring break with my friendsI. We had a great time at the Historical Museum and visiting all of the sites in Colorado Springs. Soon, it came time to return the children back to Pam.

I contacted Pam and explained to her that although we had been meeting in Dallas as the halfway point from Liberal,Ks. and Houston, actually, Wichita Falls,Texas was the correct halfway point. This was 130 miles closer for me to drive from Denver,Co. I told her that I would meet her in Wichita Falls,Tx. She said she would not even give it such a thought. She said that I would have to make the drive to Dallas because she wasn't budging and I could drive the extra miles.

So I made the drive all the way from Denver, Co., Spent the night in Liberal, Ks. then the rest of the drive on to Dallas to meet them with the children. We met at the usual spot designated. The children exited my van and had gotten into their car. To my surprise, Pam laughingly said to me, "We are on our way to Colorado to go skiing, ha,ha,ha as they sped away!" I was pretty angry to say the least! I was,however,sad for the kids for having to travel another 1000 miles unnecessarily!

I again, hired a different attorney to file a request for change of residential custody. I also, this time hired the children an attorney at $90 per hour, known as Guardian ad litem. Her job was to represent the children's best interests. A new court services officer was assigned to do the home study this time. Immediately, Pam and Herman made the 800 mile trip to Kansas to meet with this investigator as they did with the last one.

From the very first week of the order for the guardian adlidam was appointed, Pam and Herman were at their old tricks again. I had been trying to make contact with the children for a few days with no success..

My fiance, Melissa was living with me at the time who worked at a video game room at the mall. I received a phone call from her one afternoon that was rather troubling to me. She told me, "Audie and Marylin are here at the mall. They told me that they have been here at the motel and were told to stay in the room by themselves and not to contact you or they would be beaten with a belt. They have been here all week. Pam had a meeting set up with the guardian adlitem. They are going back to Texas tomorrow." I was really pissed that the children were at the attorney's office just down the street from me but could not even say hello for a minute. I also wasn't happy that I was paying for the many hours they spent there on my dime. I never had even gotten to talk to the attorney atano time throughout the duration of the court case.

The children's cries for help at times were almost too much to handle for me! Because of their cries for help, I once more took the children to a mental health professional for an evaluation in another city. The therapist there also reported in her written findings that it would be dangerous for them to return home with their mother.

These were very troubling times for the children, Meiissa and I. Every day, they would come to me while visiting my home, begging for me not to bring them back home.

The night before I was to bring them to Dallas, it was about midnight, they both came into my bedroom crying. Audie pleaded, "Please, Daddy, don't make us go back to them." I immediately decided that that was the last straw! I decided that I had one option left and that was to contact the news media for help.

The following morning, I called the local newspaper to have them come to my house. Be mindful that I did not coerce the children as to what to say nor did I even know what they were going to say to the newspaper reporter.

I was not expecting for the reporter to place our picture on the front page and a second page with a long drawn out detailed abuses. Audie and Marylin spoke freely of things that they had never even told me. It was very detailed! The next day, I received a call from the head of children's protective services locally.

After it was said and done, I don't feel that the newspaper article helped the children's case and it only made their mom and step dad to be very resentful toward the children for it. It also made the local judges very angry at me.

Pursuant to fulfill a court order, I made the trip back to Dallas. The children normally gave me a hard time on those long trips back to their home in Houston. For example, when I would stop for gas, Audie would run away from the car refusing to go any further on the trip. Marylin would have me stop, telling me that she had to use the restroom in almost every town we came to. I had to place tissue paper on the lid of the toilet every time. Most of the times, she didn't have to pee at all. I felt so sad for the children!

CHAPTER 21

Pursuit for Justice Round Four

The cycle of drama just would not let up. I am and have always been one who wanted what was best for my loved ones. It was heartbreaking to see Audie and Maryiln go through all of the drama. I was more than ever ready and willing to not pursue court filings if and when the children were not confiding in me about all the abuses for sure! Believe me, I really just wanted everyone to get along peacefully!

I did not want anymore of the expensive, highly time consuming,stressful court battles! I was spending so much money for all the legal proceedings. I had gotten into the home improvement business and was bringing in a much more money but it all went to pay lawyers. Many times I would install siding on an entire house in 100 degree weather and all of the earnings would go to the lawyers.

Many times, I would withdraw from my investments and retirement fund to pay for all of these expenses. I also got caught up into some high return schemes that a good friend talked me into. What was worse was that I had put equal amount invested into those off shore scams for each of my children so that their future would be secure. The statements showing tens of thousands of dollars were not worth the paper they were printed on!

Fast forwarding to when Audie and Maryiln were 11 and 14 years old. I received a call from Audie. He was distraught! He told me that Pam had taken a bottle of tylenol pms. He exclaimed that he had to help get his mom to the hospital! She was hospitalized for several days for the incident.

I had received a phone call sometime prior from Audie on another occasion. He informed me that he received a call from his mother who told him that she was done and she was going to take 40 valium tablets. I said to Audie, "You need to call Herman, she is married to him!" Audie replied, "I did, Herman told me to just let her do it." I then told Audie to call 911 and get the ambulance over to his mom. He did just that. They treated and released her from the emergency room at the hospital and released her back home at the time.

This agony that the kids were going through was unbearable for me to sit back and watch. It was a never ending with one thing after another happening constantly!

I hired another high priced attorney again in Liberal to file another motion for change of residential custody. This time, surely, because the kids were older and after all of the occurrences over the years that had happened should indicate to any judge that the children should not remain with their mother. I had used up all of the resources I had as far as judges were concerned locally. The court had a judge from Pratt, Ks. (130 miles) to travel to Liberal to preside over our trial.

The trial was very nerve wrenching to say the least. Pam lied to the court as to why she was in the hospital for several days. She told the court it was an illness of some sort other than the fact that she had taken a bottle of tylenol pms. The children were never present at any of the court cases. This was probably a good thing.

The judge came down on me very hard. He told me that he had never seen a father make up so many false accusations in a custody case. He said that it was far worse than the use of drugs by the kid's mom but far worse that I had gone to the news media with this case. The judge ruled that the motion for change of residential custody was once more denied. He reprimanded me that I was to be made to halt bringing the fabricated concerns to the courts. He ordered for children to reside with their mom and step dad.

I was once again very disappointed with the legal system having no concern about the abuse of our children. I just accepted the consequences as they were. The children went their way back home with Pam and Herman to Houston although they were very disappointed as to the legal system's injustice bestowed upon them.

Pam and Herman were really making the children pay for what they had told the newspaper reporter of all of the abuses done to them.

CHAPTER 22

The Pursuit for Justice Round Five

As I mentioned in the previous chapter, I really did expect the last custody court episode would have been the final attempt to persuade the legal system to listen to their concerns. Audie and Marylin weren't going to accept the judge's final ruling in the Kansas court.

Two weeks after the kids returned to Houston, one evening with no warning, to my surprise, Audie called me from Childress, Texas which is only a four hour drive from my home. He and his sixteen year old friend drove all the way from Houston to come to my house. I asked Audie why he would do such a thing as that. He replied, "I want to talk to the judge about living with you." He said that he and his friend would be at my house that night.

Later into the night, Audie and his friend showed up at my door. They were both very tired from the thirteen hour drive from Houston. They were in an old compact car that had a front wheel bearing that was in bad shape making a grinding noise. They both called it a night sleeping on my couches in the front room.

The next day, I guess Pam had contacted my attorney. Along about lunch time, he came to my house knocking on my door. My attorney was rather forceful in his words as he exclaimed to me that I must return Audie back to Houston immediately or the judge would place Audie in a juvenile facility and have me arrested. I explained to him that I didn't even know that Audie was coming and he just showed up. He told me that be wanted to talk to the judge. My attorney told me that Audie must return, for the judge would not talk to the children until they turn eighteen.

It was getting pretty close to our summer visitation anyway so I had a mechanic repair their old car and gave them cash for them to get back home. Audie was crying as they were leaving. I explained to him that he and Marylin would be back in a few weeks for the summer and could try to talk to the judge at that time.

It was so sad as I watched them disappear down the road. Audie really had a hope that he could have changed a judge's mind by talking to him. He learned at a very young age of fourteen that that's not how the system works!

The summer was here in no time. Pam had flown Audie and Marylin to the Amarillo airport at the start of summer visitation. I drove to Amarillo to pick them up to being them with me to my home in Kansas. It was always nice to see them step off the plane. Of course it was very tiring for me to drive almost two hundred miles to pick them up and two hundred miles back home each trip. We were always excited to be with each other what little time we had.

On the way home to Kansas, Audie informed me that he wanted to talk to the judge in Pratt. Marylin spoke up with a comment that she wanted to talk to the judge to tell him about the drugs and beatings as well as the taking of baths also with Herman. I told them that I would drive them to Pratt to talk to the judge.

We made the two hour drive to the Pratt county courthouse to talk to the judge. I sat in the waiting room while Audie and Marylin had gone into his chambers. Ten minutes later, the judge's office door slowly opened. Both of them had tears in their eyes as Audie told me that the judge told them that he would not talk to them until they were eighteen.

The judge didn't want to talk to them about anything at all about his ruling. We got back into the car and made the trip back home. The kids were speechless most of the way, I might add.

After we rested up for a few days, we headed off to Red River so that Audie could do some fishing with his uncle Lauren and aunt Esther. On the way, we stopped at the horse races in Raton, New Mexico.

I never was a lucky gambler but I thought I would make a few small bets riding on the horses with the worst odds. The first horse I wagered on was not a very good bet. When the starting pistol sounded, believe it or not, my horse turned around from the starting gate running the opposite direction! I obviously didn't pick a winner. However, the next one I bet on had extremely high odds. I placed a two dollar bet on this horse. I couldn't believe my eyes when he came up first place. I won $296.00! I told the kids, "Let's go on to Red River, we are leaving now!" So off we went to meet Esther and Lauren who were already there and waiting.

We had a wonderful time in the mountains in our motorhome. Our stay was one that was relaxing and bonding for us all. We started our journey home after two short days. We had a wonderful time but were ready to get back to Kansas. We returned home late the next day with no problems.

It seemed that about every day the kids would hound me wanting me to take Pam back to court. I explained to them that I had used all of the judges in Seward county in Kansas and they will have to wait until they were eighteen like the judge said.

Both being young were persistent in pursuing living with me in Kansas. They both would tell me of their mom and Herman's acts of abuse and the use of drugs and were wanting to get away from it all.

Soon, the time had come for me to bring the kids back to Texas. They were just as reluctant as ever to return. They were insisting that they did not want to return. In spite of their resistance, I met Pam and Herman at the same meeting spot in Dallas. Again, it was a heartbreaking experience!

Not many days had passed that I had received a call from Audie. He had told me that one of Herman's nephews who was visiting them (including Marylin) tried some of their mom's pot and they took a liking to it.

I about blew my top! I knew that I ran out of resources as far as judges were concerned, not wanting to talk to the children.

I only had one more option and that was to change the jurisdiction to Houston, Texas! I knew that the living conditions were not healthy for Audie and Marylin so I had to do what I thought I had to do. That was to hire an attorney in Texas to file a motion for change of custody. I did hire an attorney who was located just forty miles from the Kansas state line in Texas. He informed me that I needed to establish residence in the state of Texas in order to be legal. I rented a property, tagged my car and even got a Texas driver's license.

I was legally a Texas resident and could file the order of change of residential custody in Houston. This was a very expensive, time consuming endeavor that should have not had to occur at all.

I had just recently, within the last previous months paid the last attorney $4,000 for his services and $900 to to the attorney I had appointed by the Kansas court to represent the children also. All to no avail!

I knew that I was taking a big risk but the children would not let up pleading to me to get them away from the drugs and abuses. We would all three pray to God for his help to change the heart of the judge.

The Texas attorney who I hired was about 800 miles from Houston. He filed a motion for custody change in Houston. The order also was filed that I was to pay for the children's attorney there to represent them. The children's attorney charged $1,000.and the attorney also asked the court that all parties get tested for illegal drug usage.

The time for the big court date had arrived. I paid for a round trip airline ticket for my attorney and I, meals, motel, car rental all in the name of rescuing the children.

The very next morning, the court was in session. The judge heard the arguments from both sides. The judge at the end of the day honored our request to have all parents and the children as well, drug tested. He ordered that we do so as soon as we left the courthouse. I was ordered to pay $450 immediate cash for the evaluation of me and one child combined and Pam and Herman were to pay for theirs and the other child's drug test to be immediately after court dismissal.

Immediately after court dismissed for the day. I paid the $450 cash that I was planning to use to take the kids to Astroworld for the drug evaluation instead. I really didn't have any more money left to entertain the kids with.

The next day, we went back to court. Audie had informed me before court that his mom and Herman did not conform to the judge's orders. He told me that Pam and Herman went to a head shop and bought supplies to wash their hair and to detox their bodies instead. They did their test the next morning before court.

As we sat in the courtroom, the judge scolded me for having hired an out of county, long distance attorney to represent me. He scolded me also of making all of these accusations up. He said he has never witnessed a father fight so hard for custody of children. He told me that he was going to make it impossible to fight anymore. He denied the change of custody.

My attorney and I got into our rental car and onto the airport where we boarded the plane back to Amarillo. We then drove the remaining 100 mi.the rest of the way to Perryton.

In conclusion, this father is in hopes that my true story will be of help as a precaution of mistakes that were made in my costly, time consuming emotional roller coaster ride with the legal system. Both of the children ended up addicted to their mother's drugs. They both discovered that it had helped them with their anxiety and depression. The fact that they experimented with the drug in their home, was a life changer for them for the rest of their lives.

Both of the children were demanded by the courts to stay with their mother and step father, Audie was to stay until his sixteenth birthday.

On Audie's sixteenth birthday, he was given permission to move to Liberal, Ks. to reside with me, Marylin was to reside with her mom and step father until she was eighteen. On her eighteenth birthday, she came to live with me and presented me with this poem she had written in appreciation of my love for the two of them. Here is her heartfelt lovely poem.

Father Love
all my life I was left restrained
all those years has been refrained
now I am here!
Never shall you fear
us so nice to rejoice
and shed that joyful tear
mother, father,
love is absent apart
but all my love is like glue in my heart

I forgot not of my father's love
I shall not forget,
I shall not make love above
happy I am
happy I remain
for this is the life I have lived
it is no longer a refrain
so many years without you
love me apart
made me blue
broke my heart

I thank the lord for this wonder of a day
down to my knee to pray
was your birthday some
days ago

Brought to this earth that day
my father of mine
like was torture and a burning pain
now I rejoice, I'm healed and fine
all my life, left retrained
but with my father's love
I see again.

See my glowing face
from my forehead to my chin?
Happy birthday
father of mine
no more pain and torture
for life in now a din,
Your Mariah Marie

The End

Printed in the USA
CPSIA information can be obtained
at www.ICGtesting.com
LVHW081247210924
791739LV00041B/238

9 781955 944045

GW01246605

MIGHTY
MILITARY MACHINES

Tanks

by Matt Scheff

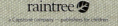

raintree
a Capstone company — publishers for children

Raintree is an imprint of Capstone Global Library Limited, a company incorporated in England and Wales
having its registered office at 264 Banbury Road, Oxford, OX2 7DY – Registered company number: 6695582

www.raintree.co.uk
myorders@raintree.co.uk

Edited by Marissa Kirkman
Designed by Heidi Thompson
Picture research by Jo Miller
Production by Tori Abraham
Originated by Capstone Global Library Ltd
Printed and bound in India

ISBN 978 1 4747 6170 3
22 21 20 19 18
10 9 8 7 6 5 4 3 2 1

British Library Cataloguing in Publication Data
A full catalogue record for this book is available from the British Library.

Acknowledgements
We would like to thank the following for permission to reproduce photographs:
Getty Images: Ed Darack, 11; Shutterstock: Simon_g, 17; U.S. Army photo by Sgt. Cody Quinn, CJTF-OIR
Public Affairs, 5, Visual Information Specialist Gertrud Zach, cover, 13; Wikimedia: U.S. Army photo by
Sgt. Aaron Ellerman, 7, Sgt. Charles Probst, 15, Staff Sgt. Michael Behlin, 19; Wikimedia: U.S. Marine Corps
photo by Gunnery Sgt. Rome M. Lazarus, 9, Master Sgt. Chad McMeen, 21

Design elements: Shutterstock: Zerbor

Contents

Tanks

What is that huge vehicle?

It is a tank!

The heavy tank rumbles over the ground.

The army uses tanks.

Jobs

Tanks are big.

They are strong and tough.

Tanks drive over

rough ground.

They fight in battles.

The crew work together to drive the tank. They sit inside the tank. The tank is noisy so the crew wear headphones.
They talk to each other using microphones.

The driver steers the tank.
The tank can drive on
soft sand.
It can drive over sharp
rocks too.

driver

Tanks have guns.

The gunner shoots the guns.

The loader helps.

They work as a team.

Parts of a tank

Tanks have armour.

It is very strong.

It keeps the crew inside the tank safe.

armour

Tanks have tracks called
caterpillar tracks.
The tracks roll over
the ground.
The tank can drive on flat
land or hills.

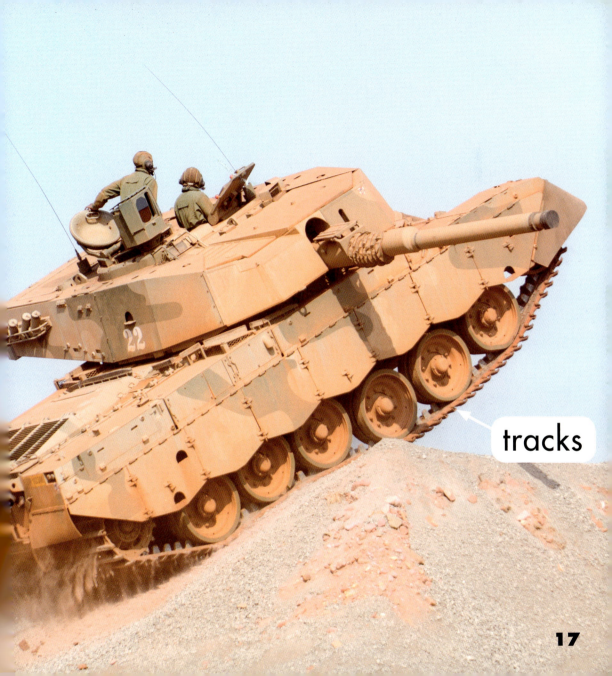

tracks

The big gun on top of the
tank is called a cannon.
The gunner shoots shells from
the cannon.
Shells are like large bullets.

Armies all over the world use tanks.
They are used in hot places and cold places.
Tanks help to protect soldiers in battles.

Glossary

armour   heavy metal layer on a military vehicle that protects against bullets or bombs

army   group of soldiers trained to fight on land

battle   fight between two different armed forces

cannon   large gun that fires large explosive shells

crew   team of people who work together

gunner   military crew member who shoots a vehicle's guns or missiles

loader   military crew member who loads a vehicle's guns or missiles

shell   large bullet fired from a cannon

tracks   piece of metal and rubber that stretches around a tank's wheels

vehicle   machines that carry people, such as cars and trains

Read more

Tanks (Ultimate Military Machines),
Tim Cooke (Wayland, 2015)

Tanks (Usborne Beginners Plus),
Henry Brook (Usborne Publishing, 2017)

Tanks (What's Inside?), David West
(Franklin Watts, 2018)

Websites

Learn more about war machines during the
First World War at:
www.bbc.co.uk/schools/0/ww1/25401270

Find out more about tanks at:
www.dkfindout.com/uk/history/world-war-i/tank-
warfare

Comprehension questions

1. Why do tanks need strong armour?

2. What jobs do the crew do inside the tank?

3. How do the tracks help a tank move?

Index